I0471089

KDP's Best-Kept Secret Revealed:

How to Embed Videos and Widgets in Your Book Description

By M. Eigh

ISBN-13: 978-1492928744
ISBN-10: 1492928747

Praises

★★★★★ "A Promise Delivered," September 24, 2013 By Maria Elizabeth Romana (NC, USA)

"I stumbled upon this book while searching for ways to enhance my books' descriptions, and what a find it was! I was so frustrated with the KDP and Author Central description systems, because I could never get even basic formatting to come out looking the way I wanted it to. This book was my answer.

"Using the information in it, I was able to re-create the book pages for several of my books and am *finally* happy with how they look (after THREE years of trying!). That said, I must warn you, it was no mean feat. It took me the better part of three days to read through and apply the material to my pages, and that was only utilizing the basic techniques; I did not include any forms, video, social media widgets, or any of the other more advanced topics. You can see examples of what I was able to do here (fiction): Little Miss Straight Lace, Book One of The Unbreakable Series (Mystery Romance Suspense) and here (non-fiction): Food, Glorious Food: The Kindle Carb & Calorie Counter, a Guide to Complete Food Counts, 2nd ed.

"I was able to accomplish this, because this book is exceptionally well-written and organized. Mr. Eigh doesn't just talk about what's possible or give you a bunch of links or vague fluff. He takes you step-by-step through the process using screenshots, examples, and clearly written text to make the process as painless as it can be. There is a lot of techno-mumbo-jumbo involved, so expect to spend some time reading, experimenting, and testing, as I did, to get quality results. If you are up to the challenge and willing to invest the time, Mr. Eigh's book will be your roadmap to a winning Kindle sales page."

★★★★★ "Great book for Kindle Marketing," September 19, 2013 By D. Ferry (Northern Virginia)

"This is a great book. It clearly took a lot of effort to discover this how-to knowledge. The presentation of the material is well-organized and straightforward. While it is helpful to know HTML and JavaScript and jQuery to use the author's ideas, it is not essential. I'm planning to use these methods for my own Kindle books. If using these methods results in just 4 or 5 sales, I will have recovered the price of Mr. Eigh's book."

★★★★★ "A Great Guide," September 28, 2013 By PGH

"Following a Goodreads discussion I was pointed at this book to help improve Product Descriptions. The methods described work, but you have to be very careful with the code as in all programming. That said, if a non-programmer, me, can do it anybody can it just takes trial and error and a bit of time to sort out. The techniques shown are excellent and certainly make the description more refreshing. Well done on an excellent guide."

★★★★★ "This is Going to Revolutionize Your Amazon Book," October 6, 2013 By CMYK "Big Wig House is a House for Busy Body ... (Indiana)

"As a programmer, I had been deeply disappointed with the lack of programming that Amazon allowed me to use when creating my books. Even some of the most standard HTML tags are ignored by Amazon formating. I felt very limited... that is until I learned about this book by Eigh. This book can help you figure out workarounds to do more with your Amazon book. Standing out in the Amazon marketplace is tough, this book holds the keys to garnering attention. I want to thank Eigh for creating this book. The knowledge inside here will take my book to a whole new level. I was living in the stone age but now thanks to this book my own Amazon books are going to into the digital age."

★★★★★ "LOVE, LOVE, This Book.." September 21, 2013 By Deb Baker "Lady Ellen" (North of Toronto, Canada)

"Being a Kindle author, I know how frustrating it can be, trying to get your books noticed. The one thing all authors agree on is that having a 'show-stopping' description section is a HUGE help.

"Marcus teaches you in this book, concisely and understandably, how to make your author's information not only stand out, but be as helpful as you can be, to assist potential buyers in deciding if your book is for them.

"And you don't have to be a coding geek, performing HTML gymnastics to use it. Save your poor brain for your writing and let this book walk you through everything you need to know to have a 'one of a kind' Amazon Author's Page.

"The best is there absolutely nothing sneaky or underhanded here. Marcus did thorough analysis on Amazon's infrastructure and inter-server communication mechanism. This is not a street vendor's trickery. It's based on profound science and Amazon's system is actually configured to support it. So win-win! You just can't beat that...

"Do yourself a favour...get this book!"

★★★★★ "KDP Descriptions On Steriods," September 11, 2013 By Kevin Humphrey (Idaho, USA)

"Just when it seemed bleak for KDP authors to be able to produce a nice description was all but dead... it's alive! But only if you know how and I'm betting 98 out of 100 Kindle authors don't know have a clue as to how to put pictures, videos, scrolling banners that link to your books and much more in their descriptions. I use some of these methods on all my descriptions now and sales went up because I stand out from my competition. It's more than I usually pay, but the payback is fast and it keeps on giving. Best KDP description book yet!"

★★★★★ "If You're a KINDLE Author, You MUST GET THIS BOOK!!," September 16, 2013 By Wordman8078

"There are a lot of people with a lot of Kindle Marketing techniques for sale that you can find somewhere for free if you really dig enough. However, this is NOT the case with this book.

"'KDP's Best-Kept Secret Revealed' is a book that is WELL WORTH THE PRICE for what it has to offer you... a worm hole into a way of making your sales page stand out from the competition. The best part is that this book is your only expense. It levels the playing field in many ways, showing you how to add videos, carousels, widgets, and photos to your book description. While this books sales page kind of takes it over the top, you can easily see EVERYTHING that you can add to your own book's sales page.

"You don't need to be a programmer to do this. The author is very complete in his descriptions of the process.

"While I JUST got the book, and am in the middle of writing an email marketing sequence, I'll be implementing this into my own book's sales pages VERY SOON!! I'm completely an utterly amazed at the brilliance of the author for discovering this technique that is completely above board.

"As a KINDLE Author, you should have this book!! That's all there is to it!!"

★★★★★ "Best Value for Your Money," September 23, 2013 By Bill Sidhu

"I just bought your book "How to Embed Videos ... in your KDP Book Description", the least i can say anything about this book is that it is worth many times the money i paid for it. I am real happy with my purchase.Hats off to you Sir - Excellent excellent job. Very useful. I am not a techie, I am actually afraid of the words like HTML, JAVA etc. etc., so it is interesting that i had just started my search to convert my book description into something more of an interesting read, rather than a plane Jan or drab looking flat document. As i have zero knowledge and time to learn even the most basic stuff much less, advanced technology to do the conversion. I stumbled into your book on Amazon and i feel that the Universe was listening to my prayers then at that time! I have already read your book and very excited to put it to use as it sounds simple enough even for a novice like me to implement it. Boy! It is a great value!Thanks for bring it out!"

Copyright Note

Caveat Emptor

By purchasing this document, you acknowledge that you are the full legal representative in your relationship with Amazon KDP. What you decide to do with your Kindle Book description is entirely your decision. You are ultimately responsible for compliance with Amazon's terms and conditions in regards to KDP.

You further acknowledge that the author of this document only provides technical know-how but does not suggest or endorse any specific applications of such know-how.

Last but not least, KDP is the most dynamic and fast-evolving playing field in Amazon's ecosystem. As past history shows, Amazon is prone to introduce sudden changes in the form of restrictions and revocations of previously granted accesses. You must acknowledge that this document reflects viable and tested technical know-how against the current set of circumstances set by Amazon in KDP. These circumstances are beyond the control of you and the author. In the unfortunate event that Amazon changes the rules of the game to such extent that this document becomes invalid partially or in its entirety, you acknowledge that such turn of events are *force majeure,* and that the author does not guarantee the permanence of the document's validity or effectiveness.

Chapter One: Why Such a Big Deal?

[If you don't care about the Why's, jump over to Chapter Four to learn the How's]

If you have to ask this question, you are probably not keenly aware of the restrictions Amazon has imposed on KDP book descriptions. Basically, you cannot use any meaningful HTML tags to enhance the styling of your description text; nor can you embed a book trailer video, a clickable hyperlink to your blog or your book's Facebook Fanpage.

If you have never attempted to do any of these, put down this book and try it now. You will fail miserably. Your carefully crafted full-HTML book description, with a trailer video, some gorgeous pictures, a fancy slideshow, and Flash widget won't pass the scrutiny of KDP Bookshelf's text editor. Your code will get stripped, sanitized and crippled. None of your pictures, trailer video, slideshow or Flash widget will render under the Book Description field on your Amazon book page. All your prospective readers will see on that book page of yours is a bunch of garbage.

But it can be done. Through a lot of investigative work and many hours spent on research, I've discovered a secret path, an undocumented backdoor to deliver your full HTML book description into your book's Product Description field.

And don't worry. This is not an illegal break-in or security vulnerability exploit. This secret backdoor has always been there. The vast majority of KDP publishers or authors just don't know of its existence. Every steps outlined in this book to help you get through this secret backdoor is just normal interaction with Amazon's book detail editing interface. It is a routine process that is subject to Amazon's normal scrutiny.

If you do not believe the existence of this backdoor, all you need to do is look at the book descriptions of my titles, including this one's own. You will see pictures, videos and slideshows, iFrames and other fancy stuff embedded inside my book descriptions.

Chapter Two: Why Bother?

You don't have to. But if you want make it easier for your prospective buyers to discover how good your book is, you pull no punch to attract their attention and seduce them to purchase your book, or at least try the free sample of your book. Unless a customer has come to Amazon to specifically look for your book, he or she is not going to spend more than 15 seconds on your book page if he or she has just stumbled on your book or randomly come across with it due to its category or search keywords.

15 seconds is a very short time. If your book cover is stunning, chances are that customer may decide to linger a bit longer. If your book has many reviews, it may also retain the customer's attention a little bit longer. He or she may decide to take a glance at the book's Book Description to get a synopsis of your book. So he or she scrolls the page down to the Description.

That's the moment a good description can make a huge difference. If you have a book trailer bearing a Play arrow, the customer instinctively wants to click on it. If the video piques his or her interest, he or she may read your synopsis more carefully. After all these steps, the customer may still lose interest quickly. (Maybe your book just does not sound like his or her cup of tea. Nothing personal.) So he or she gets ready to leave.

That's when the old "a foot in the door" sales trick kicks in. Every prospective buyer that has come to your book page is precious. You do not want to let him or her go easily. This is where you need a Flash widget that scrolls through all the other titles you have on sale. Your Flash widget resides right underneath the book synopsis and is quite "in your face" from the prospective buyer's point of view. One of your other titles may interest him or her again and he or she clicks on it and gets taken to another book page of yours.

Imagine, if you did not have the book trailer, or the Flash widget that showcases the collection of all your titles, you could have lost that customer 15 seconds ago.

And you owe it to yourself to make your book description engaging, intriguing and convincing. After all, you have written and published a book in order to sell it, for the sake of income or fame, none of which can be achieved without customers showing interest in your book and buying it.

We all know how tough it is to sell a book on Amazon. If I may paraphrase Tolstoy, all fast-selling books on Amazon have good reasons behind their popularity, while the slow-sellers or never-sellers have a million different reasons for their failures.

But if you look deeper carefully, you can identify a common malaise suffered by these failing publisher or authors – they all suffer from what I call the Cinderella Syndrome. Of all the stereotypes our parents have washed our brains with – and that we continue to employ on our own children – none is more vivid than Cinderella. When we find ourselves in a tough situation, we immediately equate ourselves with Cinderella, and we consume ourselves with indignation for the injustice upon us and a tenacious hope that the Fairy Mother will eventually show up with her magic wand.

Publishers or authors who suffer from Cinderella Syndrome believe their books are the best things since sliced bread. The reason they are not selling yet is because they have not been discovered yet. Who knows, one of these days, a top book blogger may stumble on my book and purchase a copy. He's going to post rave review. "Mark my words, this guy/gal is going to be the next [insert the name of your most admired author's name here]."

Okay, you can dream on, or you can make some effort to make it easier for people – including top reviewers, for that matter – to discover your book, by enhancing your book description with more informative, engaging features.

The technique outlined in this book provides the hands-on guide to achieve that objective.

Chapter Three: Why Go Down-and-Dirty?

Well, that is a $700K question. Let me tell you why.

As of this writing, Rick Yancey's *The 5th Wave* [Kindle Edition] ranks #1,705 Paid in Kindle Store. I think you would agree with me if I say that ranking is pretty good.

What's the sales ranking of your Kindle book? Not even close to #1,705? Well, allow me to ask you a follow-up question: have you spend $700k on marketing your Kindle book yet? Because that is the budget Penguin Group (USA) LLC has spent or is spending to promote Rick Yancy's book.

If you are reading this book, I will bet my farm that you do not have $700K to spend on promoting your book. But you can spend $9.99 to buy a copy of this book, which reveals the down-and-dirty secret on how to embed full HTML code into your Kindle book's Description field, so that it will stands out from the vast ocean of self-published e-books.

And since HTML is a visual enhancement, your book will stand out at the prospective buyer's first glance.

So why not get low down and dirty. Don't be a snub unless you have that $700K to spare on the marketing of your book.

Chapter Four: An Overview of Amazon's Book Description Rendering Engines

[If you just want to roll up your sleeves and start with embedding HTML into your book description, jump over to Chapter Five for the specific steps.]

Amazon provides two rendering engines for Kindle Book's "Book Description." One is a direct rendering engine that delivers the publisher's direct input on KDP's Book Shelf. The other is from the author or publisher's AuthorCentral Book List.

These two rendering engines for the large part bear no difference, but their mechanisms are different like night and day under the hood. A Kindle Book description, when delivered from KDP Book Shelf, is delivered from KDP's repository (database servers) directly to Amazon's Web servers. Such content flows through a tightly coupled database to a Web server and has to run through a gauntlet of filters. As a result, Amazon KDP's limited HTML tag use as well as no media embedding policy gets enforced effectively. Virtually all HTML tags that are not white-listed are stripped. It's safe to say that KDP Book Shelf is a dead alley that offers no thoroughfare, if you are trying to spice up your Book Description with fancy HTML markups.

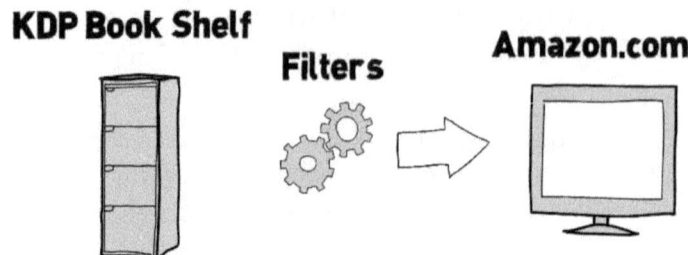

On the other hand, the Book Description delivered from AuthorCentral's Book List is *not* fetched directly from a database repository to a Web server. Instead, it is delivered from an AuthorCentral database repository to an intermediary Web server. This intermediary Web server then catalogs such Book Description in the form of HTML code blocks or snippets, by way of Web Services. Amazon's customer-facing Web servers then fetch such Book Description HTML blocks when needed, by calling the Web Service. Therefore, Book Description content, when originated from AuthorCentral, travels from one Web server to another, following the Web's cardinal protocol: http (Hypertext Transfer Protocol.)

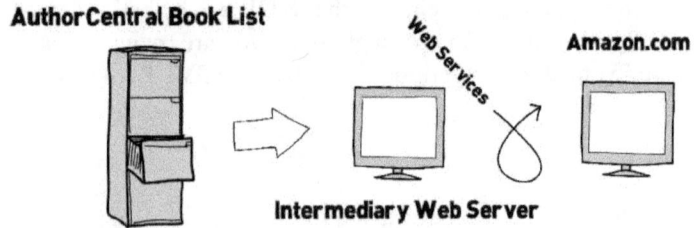

It will take another voluminous book to explain the difference in the aforementioned two mechanisms in technological terms. But for the purpose of this document, it suffices to say that this Web server-to-Web server transfer of hypertext blocks has created a loophole in Amazon's textual content delivery and rendering engine, hence giving us a great opportunity to get fancy with our Book Description.

Chapter Five: How to Embed HTML Markups in AuthorCentral Editor

This chapter assumes that you know HTML pretty well. If not, just pretend that you know it pretty well for now. Chapter Six is dedicated to people who know nothing about coding HTML.

There are no tools you need in order to embed fancy HTML markup into your AuthorCentral List Book Description, as long as you have a computer or tablet and Internet connection. I do not recommend doing it on a iPhone or other Smart Phone, mainly because neither KDP Book Shelf nor Amazon AuthorCentral Book List is optimized for mobile and many of the modal dialog boxes go out of your screen.

For demonstration purposes, we can use my own book *The Cicada Survival Guide* (http://amzn.to/19cCeFr). The Book Description panel looks like the following screenshot.

It contains an image left aligned with a descriptive block. There are some hyperlinked text (Web addresses or URL's) in the text block. Below the text block, there is a YouTube video.

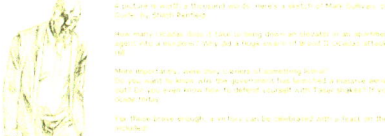

The corresponding HTML code block is as follows:

```
About the author: M. Eigh is just
another harmless Asian dude who makes a
quiet living in IT. He lives in
Northern Virginia with his beautiful
wife, two daughters and two cats in a
charming old house, which came with a
morbidly obese landlord, also known as
the mortgage. He dreams of murdering
that landlord with a bestseller someday,
preferably before he has to start
paying for the kids' colleges. His
hermit kingdom is at <a
href="//m.eigh.com">m.eigh.com</a>. <br
clear="all"><br clear="all"><img
src="//m.eigh.com/wp-
content/Mrk_by_Shiloh_Penfield.jpg"
```

align="left" border="0">
A picture
is worth a thousand words. Here's a
sketch of Mark Sullivan, one of the
main victims of Troma in <i>The Cicada
Survival Guide</i>, by Shiloh
Penfield.

How many cicadas does
it take to bring down an elevator in an
apartment building? Can a deadly cicada
turn a Secret Service agent into a
murderer? Why did a huge swarm of Brood
II cicadas attack a CIA Deputy Director
on the steps of the Capital Hill ...

More importantly, were they
carriers of something lethal?
Do you
want to know why the government has
launched a massive aerial insecticide
spray in an attipt to wipe the cicadas
out? Do you even know how to defend
yourself with Taser shakes? If you
don't, better pick up a copy of <i>The
Cicada Survival Guide</i>
today.

For those brave enough, a
victory can be celebrated with a feast
on these bugs. Delicious and battle-
tested cicada recipes
included!

Lori Milani, a.k.a.
"CicadaPhobia," has been featured in a
WashingtonPost special on Cicada on May
18. (<a href="//bit.ly/109Q621"
target="_blank">WashingtonPost's
Feature on CicadaPhobia</a>) Lori did
an extensiveinterview with the author
on May 30. For those who are interested
in how the book was conceived, please
hop over CicadaPhobia's site and
readthe interview. (<a
href="//bit.ly/11dWdQO"
target="_blank">CicadaPhobia Interviews

```
M. Eigh</a>)<br clear="all"><h2>Do you
say si-KAY-da? Or si-KAH-da? Watch Zoe
and Jennifer debate in this
video:</h2><div align="center"><iframe
src="//youtube.com/embed/9wJOXiIQS7c?fe
ature=player_detailpage"
allowfullscreen="" frameborder="0"
height="360"
width="640"></iframe></div><script
type="text/JavaScript"
src="//sk2000inc.com/misc/jquery.js"></
script><script
type="text/JavaScript">$(document).read
y(function(){amz_expandPostBodyDescript
ion('PS', ['psGradient',
'psPlaceHolder']);});</script><br
clear="all"><br clear="all">
```

Our job now is to input the above code block into Amazon AuthorCentral Book List's Rich Text Editor. However, if we just put the above HTML block into the Rich Text Editor in AuhtorCentral, the majority of all the HTML tags will be stripped by the editor's sanitizer. As a result, the censored leftover code will be unusable and when rendered on Amazon.com, it will be a total mess.

To bypass the sanitizer, we must first double-encode our HTML. Double encoding HTML basically means that the open bracket "<" will be turned into "<" and the close bracket will be ">." A typical "<script>" tag will therefore be disguised as "<script>," hence fooling the sanitizer into giving the code block a green light. If you are an HTML guru and are feeling heroic, you are welcome to do the double encoding by hand. But it is totally unnecessary and error prone.

Technically, the so-called double encoding process is called "HTML encoding." There are tons of free HTML encoders available online for you to download and install on your computer or device. As a matter of fact, since the HTML code block you are using for Book Description is guaranteed to be small (Amazon imposes a 4000 character limit on the Description field,) the easiest way to get the HTML encoding process done is to find a online HTML encoder and do it through a Web form. If you just Google "online HTML encoder," you should be able to find many choices. But my favorite is located at http://www.opinionatedgeek.com/DotNet/Tool s/HTMLEncode/Encode.aspx. The following screenshot shows you how my entire book description HTML block gets double encoded with this online encoder:

Type or paste in the text you want to HTML encode, then press the 'Encode' button, or read a brief explanation of the process of HTML encoding.

Encode input text:

```
in IT. He lives in Northern Virginia with his
beautiful wife, two daughters and two cats in
a charming old house, which came with a
morbidly obese landlord, also known as the
mortgage. He dreams of murdering that landlord
with a bestseller someday, preferably before
he has to start paying for the kids' colleges.
His hermit kingdom is at <a
href="//m.eigh.com">m.eigh.com</a>. <br
clear="all"/><br clear="all"/><img
src="//m.eigh.com/wp-
content/Mrk_by_Shiloh_Penfield.jpg" border="0"
align="left" /><br />A picture is worth a
thousand words. Here's a sketch of Mark
Sullivan, one of the main victims of Troma in
<i>The Cicada Survival Guide</i>, by Shiloh
```

Don't forget to check out out online HTML Decoder.

Encode

Encoded Output

Here is the HTML-encoded output:

```
 About the author: M. Eigh is just another
harmless Asian dude who makes a quiet living
in IT. He lives in Northern Virginia with his
beautiful wife, two daughters and two cats in
a charming old house, which came with a
morbidly obese landlord, also known as the
mortgage. He dreams of murdering that landlord
with a bestseller someday, preferably before
he has to start paying for the kids&#39;
colleges. His hermit kingdom is at &lt;a
href=&quot;//m.eigh.com&quot;&gt;m.eigh.com&lt;
/a&gt;. &lt;br
clear=&quot;all&quot;/&gt;&lt;br
clear=&quot;all&quot;/&gt;&lt;img
src=&quot;//m.eigh.com/wp-
content/Mrk_by_Shiloh_Penfield.jpg&quot;
```

After the double coding, my book description HTML block becomes humanly unreadable. But don't fret. If you can't read it, Amazon can't strip it. Mine looks like the following block:

```
About the author: M. Eigh is just
another harmless Asian dude who makes a
quiet living in IT. He lives in
Northern Virginia with his beautiful
wife, two daughters and two cats in a
charming old house, which came with a
morbidly obese landlord, also known as
the mortgage. He dreams of murdering
that landlord with a bestseller someday,
preferably before he has to start
paying for the kids&#39; colleges. His
hermit kingdom is at &lt;a
href=&quot;//m.eigh.com&quot;&gt;m.eigh
.com&lt;/a&gt;. &lt;br
clear=&quot;all&quot;/&gt;&lt;br
clear=&quot;all&quot;/&gt;&lt;img
src=&quot;//m.eigh.com/wp-
content/Mrk_by_Shiloh_Penfield.jpg&quot
; border=&quot;0&quot;
align=&quot;left&quot; /&gt;&lt;br
/&gt;A picture is worth a thousand
words. Here&#39;s a sketch of Mark
Sullivan, one of the main victims of
Troma in &lt;i&gt;The Cicada Survival
Guide&lt;/i&gt;, by Shiloh
Penfield.&lt;br /&gt;&lt;br /&gt;How
many cicadas does it take to bring down
an elevator in an apartment building?
Can a deadly cicada turn a Secret
Service agent into a murderer? Why did
a huge swarm of Brood II cicadas attack
a CIA Deputy Director on the steps of
the Capital Hill ... &lt;br /&gt;&lt;br
```

/>More importantly, were they carriers of something lethal?
Do you want to know why the government has launched a massive aerial insecticide spray in an attipt to wipe the cicadas out? Do you even know how to defend yourself with Taser shakes? If you don't, better pick up a copy of <i>The Cicada Survival Guide</i> today.

For those brave enough, a victory can be celebrated with a feast on these bugs. Delicious and battle-tested cicada recipes included!

Lori Milani, a.k.a. "CicadaPhobia," has been featured in a WashingtonPost special on Cicada on May 18. (<a href="//bit.ly/109Q621" target="_blank" >WashingtonPost's Feature on CicadaPhobia</a>) Lori did an extensiveinterview with the author on May 30. For those who are interested in how the book was conceived, please hop over CicadaPhobia's site and readthe interview. (<a href="//bit.ly/11dWdQO" target="_blank" >CicadaPhobia Interviews M. Eigh</a>)<br clear="all"/><h2>Do you say si-KAY-da? Or si-KAH-da? Watch Zoe and Jennifer debate in this video:</h2><div align="center"><iframe width="640"

```
height=&quot;360&quot;
src=&quot;//youtube.com/embed/9wJOXiIQS
7c?feature=player_detailpage&quot;
frameborder=&quot;0&quot;
allowfullscreen&gt;&lt;/iframe&gt;&lt;/
div&gt;&lt;script
type=&quot;text/JavaScript&quot;
src=&quot;//sk2000inc.com/misc/jquery.j
s&quot;&gt;&lt;/script&gt;&lt;script
type=&quot;text/JavaScript&quot;&gt;$(d
ocument).ready(function(){amz_expandPos
tBodyDescription(&#39;PS&#39;,
[&#39;psGradient&#39;,
&#39;psPlaceHolder&#39;]);});&lt;/scrip
t&gt;
```

Once we have this block of gibberish in hand, we are ready to go into our AuthorCentral account and follow the following steps to get the HTML embedding done.

1. Log into your Amazon Author Central Account. Drill down your book list and choose the target book. If you have multiple formats of the same book, make sure you only select the Kindle version. Fancy HTML embedding only works with Kindle Book Description. Do not try to replicate this technique in your paperback or audio formats of the book.
2. Once the Kindle format book detail page loads, click on Product Description to edit:

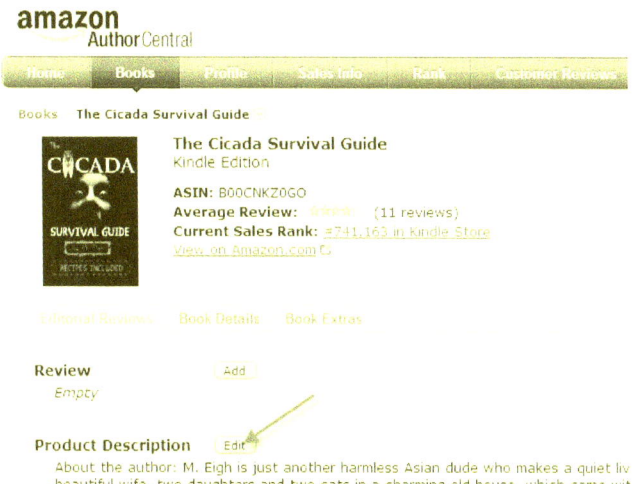

3. When the Rich Text Editor loads, make sure the "Compose" Tab is active. *Do not* use the HTML tab:

Edit review close ⓧ

Guidelines
If you are copying and pasting text from another text editing program, we recommend you use only a plain text editor like Notepad. Rich text editors like Microsoft Word often cause formatting issues which delay or prevent your request from processing.

What "Product Description" should include:

- An objective summary of the book's subject matter and genre. Think of the content on the back cover of most books.
- Up to 2400 characters (about 480 words)

What "Product Description" should not include:

- Spoilers! please don't reveal crucial plot elements.
- Phone numbers, mail addresses, URLs.

Important: Once you make a change to a section here, your publisher will not be able to make any further changes to the same section. If you are a Kindle Direct Publishing author, and you make changes to your Product Description here, you will no longer be able to make edits via KDP.

More details on "Product Description" guidelines here ⌐.

COMPOSE   EDIT HTML

Format: **B** *I* ≣ ☰

About the author: M. Eigh is just another harmless Asian dude who makes a quiet living in IT. He lives in Northern Virginia with his beautiful wife, two daughters and two cats in a charming old house, which came with a morbidly obese landlord, also known as the mortgage. He dreams of murdering that landlord with a bestseller someday, preferably before he has to start paying for the kids'

4. Paste the content of gibberish block into the editor input panel. Try your best to *not* introduce any white space or line breaks. Paste the block verbatim. Also please make sure there is no left-over code from your previous description.

5. Once code is pasted in, the description will look funny. Do not be alerted or worried. It's just a step in the process:

Important: Once you make a change to a section here, your publisher will not be able to make any further changes to the same section. If you are a Kindle Direct Publishing author, and you make changes to your Product Description here, you will no longer be able to make edits via KDP.

More details on "Product Description" guidelines here ☐.

Format: **B** *I* ≔ ≔

colleges. His hermit kingdom is at <a href=".m eigh.com".>m eigh.com<.a>. <.br clear="all".><.br clear="all".><.img src=" m.eigh.com.wp-content.Mrk_by_Shiloh_Penfield.jpg" border="0" align="left".><.br.>A picture is worth a thousand words. Here&=39;s a sketch of Mark Sullivan, one of the main victims of Troma in <i>The Cicada Survival Guide<.i>. by Shiloh Penfield.<.br.><.br.>How many cicadas does it take to bring down an elevator in an apartment building? Can a deadly cicada turn a Secret Service agent into a murderer? Why did a huge swarm of Brood II cicadas attack a CIA Deputy Director on the steps of the Capital Hill .. <.br.><.br.>More importantly, were they carriers of something lethal?<.br.>Do you want to know why the government has launched a massive aerial insecticide spray in an attipt to wipe the cicadas out? Do you even know how to defend yourself with Taser shakes? If you don&=39;t, better pick up a copy of <i>The Cicada Survival Guide<.i> today.<.br.><.br.>For those brave enough, a victory can be celebrated with a feast on these bugs. Delicious and battle-tested cicada recipes included!<.br.><.br.>Lori Milani, a.k.a. "CicadaPhobia," has been featured in a WashingtonPost special on Cicada on May 18. (<a href=".bit.ly.1090621" target=".blank".

Preview ◗

6. Click on the "Preview" button and you'll notice the description block turns itself into HTML markup. Do not worry. This is normal. From now on, your Kindle Book Description inside your AuthorCentral Control Panel will look like this. But this is just the internal view. It will be quite different in the Amazon book page:

Preview your review close ⊠

🔘 **Your changes have not yet been saved**
Please review your content and click 'Save changes' to continue.

About the author: M. Eigh is just another harmless Asian dude who makes a quiet living in IT. He lives in Northern Virginia with his beautiful wife, two daughters and two cats in a charming old house, which came with a morbidly obese landlord, also known as the mortgage. He dreams of murdering that landlord with a bestseller someday, preferably before he has to start paying for the kids' colleges. His hermit kingdom is at <a href="//m.eigh.com">m.eigh.com</a>. <br clear="all"/><br clear="all"/><img src="//m.eigh.com/wp-content/Mrk_by_Shiloh_Penfield.jpg" border="0" align="left" />
A picture is worth a thousand words. Here's a sketch of Mark Sullivan, one of the main victims of Troma in <i>The Cicada Survival Guide</i>, by Shiloh Penfield.

How many cicadas does it take to bring down an elevator in an apartment building? Can a deadly cicada turn a Secret Service agent into a murderer? Why did a huge swarm of Brood II cicadas attack a CIA Deputy Director on the steps of the Capital Hill ...

More importantly, were they carriers of something lethal?
Do you want to know why the government has launched a massive aerial insecticide spray in an attipt to wipe the cicadas out? Do you even know how to defend yourself with Taser shakes? If you don't, better pick up a copy of <i>The Cicada Survival Guide</i> today.

For those brave enough, a victory can be celebrated with a feast on these bugs. Delicious and battle-tested cicada recipes included!

Lori Milani, a.k.a. "CicadaPhobia," has been featured in a WashingtonPost special on Cicada on May 18. {<a href="//bit.ly/109Q621" target="_blank" >WashingtonPost's Feature on CicadaPhobia</a>} Lori did an extensiveinterview with the author on May 30. For those who are interested in how the book was conceived, please hop

 Go back   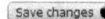 Save changes 🔘

7. Click on "Save" and wait at least 30 minutes.
8. Go back and see the change in your Book Description on the Amazon Product page.

Chapter Six: How to Code Your Book Description in HTML

Skip this chapter if you are familiar with HTML. This is intended for people who do not have any clue about HTML – not that there's anything wrong with that.

The most intuitive way of turning your book description into HTML is to write it in Word, then save the Word document as "HTML Web page (filtered)." However, I do not recommend this route. A Microsoft Word document, when saved as HTML, retains a great deal of proprietary inline styling, hence bringing about damages on two levels: 1) It forces Microsoft's proprietary styling onto your description block and makes it look like the odd man out when inside an Amazon book page. 2) The Product Description field has a 4000 character max. The granular, excessive inline styling code itself quickly eats up the quota and you will not be able to fit any meaningful description into your Description field.

Instead, simply use your favorite Web email composer as your HTML editor. Suppose you want your book description to read as follows:

This Is a Book

Paragraph one

Paragraph two

   1. One

   2. Two

   3. Three

Paragraph three. "Quoted content."|

Follow the steps as follows to get the proper HTML code from your Web email composer. We will use Gmail as an example.

- Use FireFox as your browser and log into your Gmail account's Web interface. Launch the composer modal dialog box.
- Write a description. The following screenshot is a simple example:

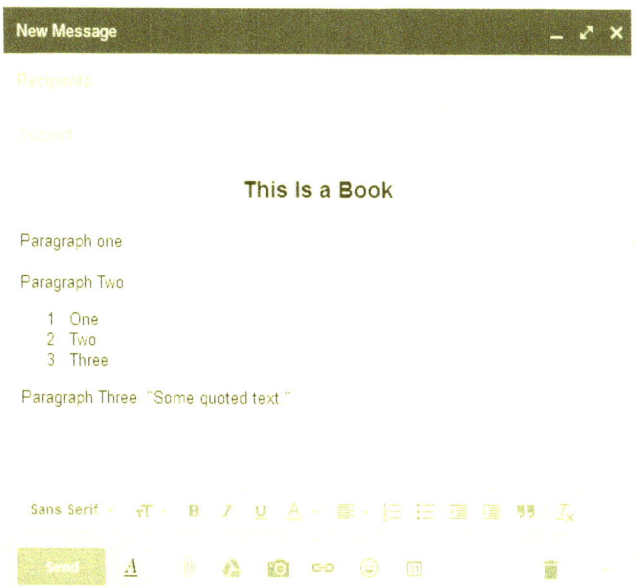

- If you need a picture to be part of the description, make sure the picture is available on the Web. Copying a picture from your local computer or device will not work. So copy your desired picture from the Web (from Google Image, your own Flickr photo and etc.)

- Simply paste the picture into your
  composer, at a desired location:

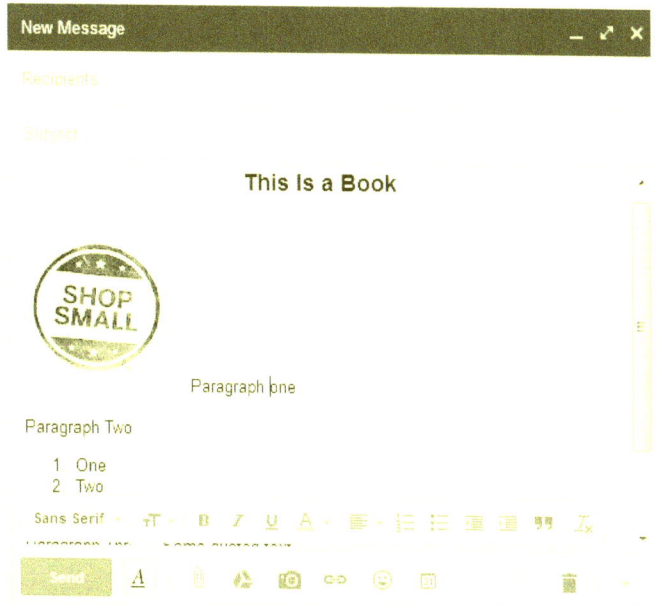

- Now select the entire block of your book description and make sure the picture is part of the selection. While the selection is active, right click and choose "View selection source." Make sure you use FireFox as your browser. Other browsers either do not give you this option or their ways are more cumbersome:

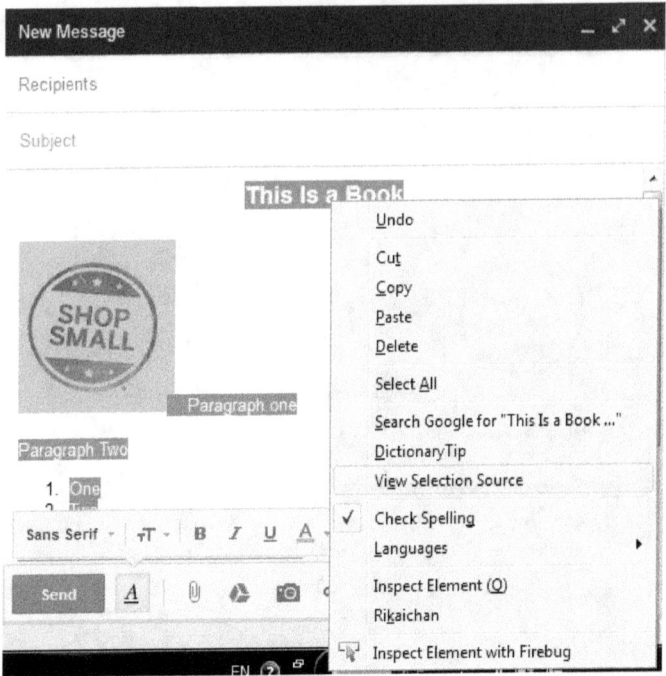

- Now the HTML code block representing your book description will be in the popped up source view window:

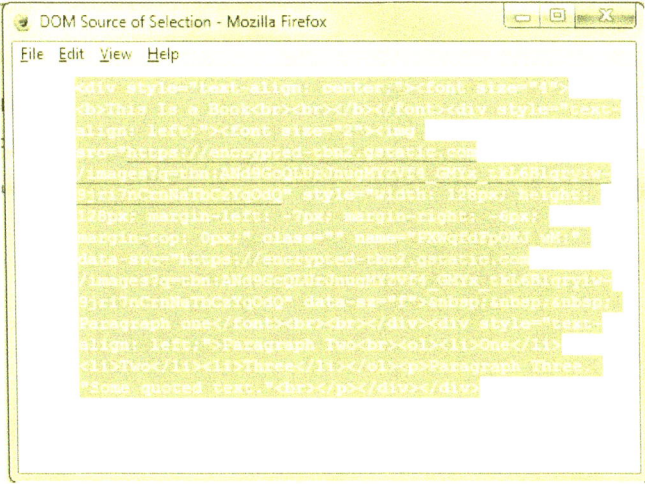

- Copy the source code somewhere in a text file. There you have it, your pre-double encoding HTML code block, courtesy of Gmail.

Chapter Seven: How to Obtain Video Embed Code Block

This is probably the easiest part of the whole process. We will use YouTube as an example. Most other video service providers have a similar mechanism that makes easy for you to obtain the embedding code.

Go to the YouTube video you want to embed. Right click on the video screen and select "Copy embed code." Open Notepad or any other text editor and paste the code somewhere.

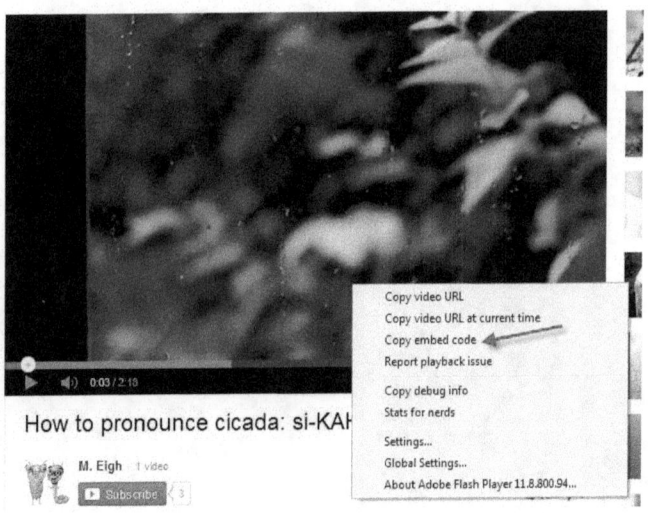

The above example's embed code looks like the following:

```
<iframe width="640" height="360"
src="http://www.youtube.com/embed/9wJOX
```

```
iIQS7c?feature=player_detailpage"
frameborder="0"
allowfullscreen></iframe>
```

Once you have the embed code, combine it with the text block HTML you have obtained via Gmail and you have got yourself a beautiful multimedia fancy HTML book description block. Now, follow the steps outlined in Chapter Five to get into delivered into your Book Description field.

Make a note here: The aforementioned YouTube code block cannot be used verbatim. The code block contains a URL protocol prefix "http:" which must be stripped before the block can be put in AuthorCentral Editor's Compose tab; otherwise the valid YouTube URL will be sanitized your embedded video will become a blank screen. If we preemptively stripped the URL protocol prefix, our embed code block becomes Amazon-ready, as follows:

```
<iframe width="640" height="360"
src="//www.youtube.com/embed/9wJOXiIQS7
c?feature=player_detailpage"
frameborder="0"
allowfullscreen></iframe>
```

This no-prefix rule for URLs must be observed at all time for your description block to bypass AuthorCentral Editor's built-in sanitization. It is further explained in Chapter Eight.

Chapter Eight: Pitfalls to Watch For

When you are embedding fancy HTML into the AuthorCentral Book List Editor, there are two missteps that can wreak havoc. One is the accidental or erroneous white spaces, the other is the accidental or erroneous line breaks. Both of these will ruin your book description and may even render them completely unreadable.

To avoid these pitfalls, always be conscious of the code block's fidelity. Always use plain text editor as opposed to a rich text editor for copying and pasting, and storing HTML code blocks. For example, always use Notepad instead of Wordpad or Word.

Notepad is not a perfect choice either, as it sometimes introduces arbitrary line breaks and destroys your code.

The best free text editor on the market that retains the fidelity of your code block's white spaces and line breaks is Notepad++, a freeware. Give it a try.

The other major pitfall to watch is the common URL prefix. Since you are dealing with HTML and therefore must embed hyperlinks – you know, when you want to embed a link to your own blog in your book description, or when you have to reference an image in your Flickr account.

A standard URL bears a prefix to suggest its transfer protocol. Google's URL, for example, is `http://ww.google.com`.

But if you want to be able to pass a URL into your book description, you can *never* prefix a URL with "http://." Amazon's sanitizer watches for this particular string in your input, and strips it off whenever it's encountered. As a result, if you are linking to http://www.google.com, the link will become www.google.com. This will basically render the link not clickable or dead. Imagine if you are using a link in your video embedding code to refer to YouTube as – for example – http://www.youtube.com/watch?v=9wJOXiIQS7c. It will become www.youtube.com/watch?v=9wJOXiIQS7c and your video will become a permanent blank screen.

To counter this URL prefix block, you must prefix every Web URL as "//" instead of "http://." As a result, Google's URL will be "//www.google.com" instead of "http://www.google.com."

Therefore, The abovementioned YouTube URL is then "//www.youtube.com/watch?v=9wJOXiIQS7c."

Last but not least, if you know HTML and JavaScript well and like to use a lot of JavaScript in your description, watch out for the single quote or apostrophe. For example, the following line uses single quote and looks better than double quote from a coder's perspective:

```
var myBook = 'This is a book.'
```

However, for the purpose of embedding this line of JavaScript into your book's description, you are better off replacing the single quote with straight double quote. (Avoid fancy double quote such as Microsoft Word-generated curly quote.)

```
var myBook = "This is a book. "
```

Chapter Nine: A Final Warning

You can use the afore-introduced technique to do other segments of your book page, such as "Review," "From the Author," "About the Author" and etc. You can use fancy HTML as well.

However, if you are an author who cares to a great deal the sales of your books in marketplaces other than Amazon.com, you need to exercise caution when allocating descriptive elements to fields other than Product Description in AuthorCentral. Whatever you enter in those fields, be it From the Author or About the Author, they will always show up on Amazon.com; however, the same fields other than the default Description may not show up on the following Amazon marketplaces:

- Amazon.co.uk
- Amazon.in
- Amazon.de
- Amazon.fr
- Amazon.es
- Amazon.it
- Amazon.co.jp
- Amazon.com.br
- Amazon.ca
- Amazon.com.mx

Generally speaking, if you do care about other marketplaces than Amazon.com, use Description field as the central repository for your most important sales pitch. Use other fields such as From the Author or About the Author for nonessential or "optional" descriptive elements.

If you need to test the appearance of a specific descriptive field on your book page when loaded on an Amazon marketplace other than Amazon.com, you can go by the URL switching rule as follows:

All Amazon ebooks follow a URL pattern as http://www.amazon.com/dp/ASIN. For example, this book you are reading has "B00F23Q9CI" as its ASIN and hence its Amazon.com's permanent URL is as follows:

http://www.amazon.com/dp/ B00F23Q9CI

If I need to find out how my book description looks on Amazon.co.uk, all I need to do is to replace ".com" with ".co.uk" and load the URL in a browser, as follows:

http://www.amazon.co.uk/dp/ B00F23Q9CI

Amazon in Germany would then be:

http://www.amazon.de/dp/ B00F23Q9CI

And so on so forth.

In addition to the standard 4000-character limit, you must remember this technique *only* works with the Book Details of the Kindle format of your book. Not only does it not work with that of your paperback format, your Book Description will actually render the raw HTML directly if you try to embed HTML blocks into your paperback version.

Chapter Ten: Advanced Book Description Hacks

This chapter is intended for people with advanced HTML and JavaScript experience. If you are a beginner in terms of HTML and JavaScript, you should attempt these advanced hacks with the help of an experienced front-end Web developer; or, contact me directly for help at eigh.com@gmail.com.

The advanced hacks often used are fairly hard to categorize. As a result, I am just going to list them one by one in a laundry list, by descending order of most frequently used to the least.

How to auto-expand the Kindle book Description field when your book page loads:

A typical default behavior of a Kindle book Book Description field is "folded" when the page first loads. Using my own book *Bitter Tea and Braided Hair* (http://amzn.to/136nIdT) as an example, the folded Description looks like the screenshot below:

Book Description
Publication Date: **May 4, 2013**

This collection packs eight exquisite short fiction from M. Eigh, including Bitter Tea and Braided Hair, My Mother's Sha Extraordinary Life, Planned, Dear Teresa, The Manchurian Express, A Eulogy for Edwin Bogardus, Not A Bad Day and D

All of the stories have been previously published by very selective professional or semi-professional literary magazines been re-printed since their first publication.

Read a recently published short fiction by M. Eigh:

˅ Show more

It has a "Show more" link at the bottom left. Once that link is clicked, the Book Description panel expands to its maximum, as shown below:

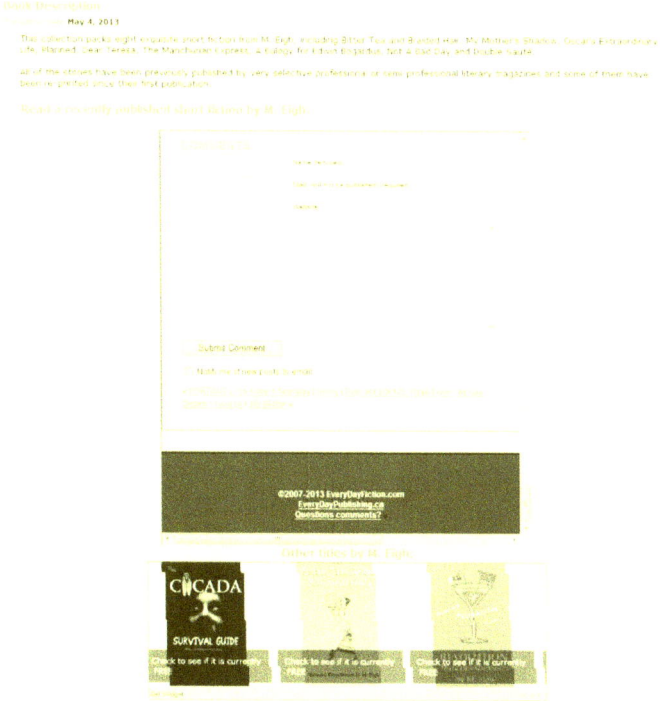

It's debatable whether you should keep it folded or expanded. I follow the Web's 3-15 usability principle – that nothing should take more than 3 clicks to get to and nothing should take more than 15 seconds to load. Given that most visitors have already spent two clicks to get to your book page – one click to get to the list view of books in the relevant group or category and another on your book's cover image when the visitor decides to check it out – I'd like to save the last click from the visitor to "Look inside," or "Send sample now," or – if I'm lucky enough – the "Buy" button.

If you prefer to keep it folded, you do not need to do anything fancy. Amazon book page's default behavior is to have the Description panel folded.

However, if you are like me and would like to have the Description panel extended, you need to follow the following steps to get it done.

1) Add a jQuery framework reference. jQuery must be hosted somewhere on the Web, preferably by a CDN optimized network such as Google. Using Google hosted jQuery as an example, the JavaScript reference should look like this:

```
<script
src="//ajax.googleapis.com/ajax/libs
/jquery/1.2.6/jquery.min.js"></scrip
t>
```

This reference block should be free of linebreaks. (It should be on one line) You also must remember to construct the GoogleAPI URL as //ajax.googleapi.com, not http://ajax.googleapi.com or else the reference will be stripped by Amazon editor's built-in sanitizer.

Right after you establish the jQuery reference, you can call a native Amazon defined JavaScript function "amz_expandPostBodyDescription()." The function takes some parameters and must be called as follows to trigger the expansion when the book page loads:

```
<script
src//ajax.googleapis.com/ajax/libs/j
query/1.2.6/jquery.min.js"></script>
<script
type="text/JavaScript">$(document).r
eady(function(){amz_expandPostBodyDe
scription('PS', ['psGradient',
'psPlaceHolder']);});</script>
```

Simply add the above code block to the bottom of your pre-double encoding HTML description. Follow steps outlined in Chapter Five and you will see your book description expanded when your book page loads.

Make a note here: There are multiple versions of jQuery framework library out there. What we need to leverage is very tiny bit of the framework's very powerful resource. In principle, you should reference a version as low as possible. The version shown here, Build 1.2.6 is tested to be working.

jQuery has undergone major changed around Version 1.9 and Amazon's JavaScript SDK has not quite caught up with the changes, as of my last check at the time of this writing. As a result, if you use Version 1.9 or Version 1.10 as your jQuery reference, your book description panel may demonstrate unpredictable behavior. So stick with Version 1.8 and under, if you can.

Use an Amazon Affiliate Flash Widget to interlink all your book title and place it at the bottom of your book description

As I mentioned before, traffic is the most precious thing to your book page. When someone hangs out on your book page, he or she's already got one foot in the door. You don't want them to leave that easily. I typically go in my Amazon Affiliate account and build a carousel that includes all my books

Amazon Widget wizard allows you to add a comment when building a carousel. I normally add "Check to see if it is currently FREE" and make it more compelling for the visitors to click on another book of mine. This is particularly useful when you have a Kindle book on free promotion. One cannot expect a high percentage of return, but it is likely that a small percentage of the visitors chasing a free book of yours will also check out one of your non-freebies, or try its sample or even buy it outright.

Plus, you would rather have them click on one of your links before they wander to some other part of Amazon, as all your book links would naturally have your Amazon Affiliate ID embedded in the URL. If a visitor clicks on one of your books in the carousel, then leaves from that book page to browse the electronics and ends up buying a $1000 TV, you get paid an advertising fee. (Even if it is just 4%, it still amounts to $40, which beats the royalty of selling 100 copies of $0.99 Kindle books.)

One advice I would like to offer is to save that carousel widget in your Affiliate account. If you are a prolific writer, you will push out more titles in the future. When a new title is added, you only need to go in your Affiliate account and add that new title to the existing widget. The code for the carousel in your book description does not need to change at all.

The embed code of Amazon Affiliate widget can be obtained in a way similar to what has been described in Chapter Seven.

    i)   Log in your Amazon Affiliate account and activate the "Widget" tab. If you have not created your widget yet, it is easy to create one from scratch.

    ii)   From the left-side Widgets panel, click on "My Widgets."

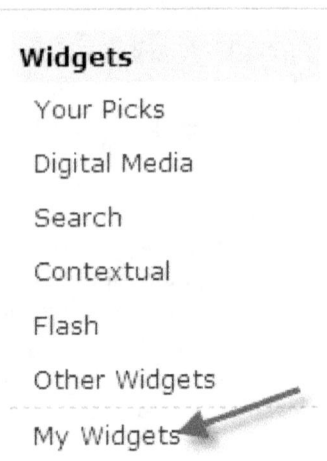

iii)   Locate your desired a widget and click on the "Get Code" button and popup window will display the code snippet:

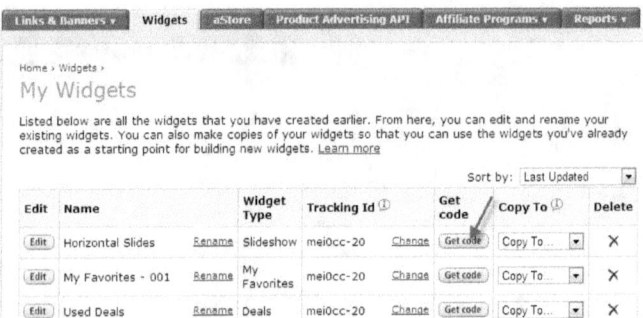

iv)   Now you can copy the code block and incorporate it into your HTML book description block:

Click the Copy button below to copy and then paste it into your Web page

```
<SCRIPT charset="utf-8" type="text/javascript" src="http://wa-
na.amazon-adsystem.com/widgets/q?
ServiceVersion=20070822&MarketPlace=US&ID=V20070822%2FUS%2Fmeiloo-
20%2F8003%2F0334e494-0210-453c-a426-
74153e6132a2&Operation=GetScriptTemplate"> </SCRIPT> <NOSCRIPT><A
HREF="http://wa-na.amazon-adsystem.com/widgets/q?
ServiceVersion=20070822&MarketPlace=US&ID=V20070822%2FUS%2Fmeiloo-
20%2F8003%2F0334e494-0210-453c-a426-
74153e6132a2&Operation=NoScript">Amazon.com Widgets</A></NOSCRIPT>
```

Copy ⬅ ——

v)   You must remember to get rid of the http protocol prefix of the URL's, or else the URL's will be sanitized and crippled. And your carousel will not render:

Click the Copy button below to copy and then paste it into your Web page

```
<SCRIPT charset="utf-8" type="text/javascript" src="http://wa-
na.amazon-adsystem.com/widgets/q?
ServiceVersion=20070822&MarketPlace=US&ID=V20070822%2FUS%2Fmeiloo-
20%2F8003%2F0334e494-0210-453c-a426-
74153e6132a2&Operation=GetScriptTemplate"> </SCRIPT> <NOSCRIPT><A
HREF="http://wa-na.amazon-adsystem.com/widgets/q?
ServiceVersion=20070822&MarketPlace=US&ID=V20070822%2FUS%2Fmeiloo-
20%2F8003%2F0334e494-0210-453c-a426-
74153e6132a2&Operation=NoScript">Amazon.com Widgets</A></NOSCRIPT>
```

Copy

The use of an iFrame and its pros and cons

Since Amazon AuthorCentral detail fields all impose a 4000-character limit, iFrame becomes handy when you need to display a huge chunk of externally hosted content. If you look at this book's description, you will notice that I have placed a "Question on KDP's Best-Kept Secret Revealed" form for prospective buyers to send their inquiries to me. This form cannot be constructed inside an AuthorCentral description field on two accounts: First, it contains a lot of HTML and JavaScript code and therefore a lot of string characters and may therefore run my book description over the 4,000 char limit. Secondly, the form needs to be submitted and handled by a server and there is no way Amazon will work with me and collect the submitters' data and relay them to me.

So I have got myself a perfect candidate for an iFrame.

iFrames are extremely easy to use and the code is bare minimal. All you need to specify is an external URL to the iFrame's "src" tag and it will render for you seamlessly in a browser, under the disguise of the hosting page. (In this case, my book page served on Amazon.)

My external URL is a simple sign-up form I have pre-generated with MailChimp. It is located at http://eigh.us7.list-manage.com/subscribe?u=59d05a6d4bf1077b2c3a8eaae&id=85d357fd50.

Before I plug that URL into an iFrame, as always, I need to strip off the "http:" protocol string. After the stripping, the URL is Amazon-sanitizer safe, as follows:

```
//eigh.us7.list-
manage.com/subscribe?u=59d05a6d4bf1077b2c3
a8eaae&id=85d357fd50
```

Which gets plugged into an iFrame and the entire form's code looks as follows:

```
<iframe src="//eigh.us7.list-
manage.com/subscribe?u=59d05a6d4bf1077b2c3
a8eaae&id=85d357fd50" width="660"
height="800"></iframe>
```

After I incorporate this iFrame block into my book description, double encode it and enter it into the AuthorCentral book description field, I beget myself a functional and seamlessly integrated signup or opt-in form, courtesy of MailChimp. (Well, don't forget there is about 30 minutes processing time on the AuthorCentral servers. Don't panic if you do not see the iFrame showing up right away on your book page.

(You will need to use this form for the first time when you ask questions.)
(**Please review the FAQ before you send a question**.)

Question on "KDP's Best-Kept Secret"

Thanks for dropping by. Please use the following form to send me a message if you have a question for me. Of course, you are more than welcome to start a forum discussion with your question. Either way, I will leave no questions unanswered.

The form submit button says "Subscribe to list" in lieu of "Submit" or "Send" because I need to filter out spammers. My own email address will be sent to you in the confirmation email. Upon receipt of that email, you do not have to confirm. You can just send a PM to my email address included there. But hopping on the list will allow you to "overhear" my answers to other people's questions. I look forward The form submit button says "Subscribe to list" in lieu of "Submit" or "Send" because I need to filter out spammers. My own email address will be sent to you in the confirmation email. Upon receipt of that email, you do not have to confirm. You can just send a PM to my email address included there. But hopping on the list will allow you to "overhear" my answers to other people's questions. I look forward to hearing from you. Cheers. M. Eigh

* indicates required

Email Address

*

First Name

Question

*

Subscribe to list

MailChimp

Since iFrames seem so agile and powerful, some of you may be tempted to use it for everything. Or even the entire book description hosted on an external server of which you have complete control. Technically and technologically speaking, there is nothing preventing you from doing that, but you need to watch for the following cons that come with iFrames:

a) When a visitor interact with the "framed" page (the page residing at the external URL you have plugged into the iFrame's "src" tag,) it is contained in that page and the hosting page – your book's page on Amazon – is completely unaware of the data transaction. This can become really awkward when a user clicks on an external link on the "framed" page and finds the new page inside an Amazon page. For example, if your "framed" description page links to a GoodReads review on your book and a user clicks on it, fully expecting to go to GoodReads, he or she will be surprised to see a partial GoodReads page shoveled inside an Amazon page. This does not help build trust between the book page and the visitors and may drive them away.

As a general rule of thumb, when you do have hyperlinked URLs on the "framed" page, the "target" attribute of the anchor tag, a.k.a., <a href= "…" target= "…" >some URL </a>, should always be specified as "_blank" or "_new." This effectively forces the visitors' browsers to open any link on the "framed" page in a new browser tab (or window, if a visitor is using a very old browser that does not support tab.)

Suppose you have a link to Google on the "framed page for some reason. That link's source code should look as follows:

```
<a href="//www.google.com" target=
"_new" >www.google.com</a>
```

b) Performance lag. Amazon is a giant and has the infrastructure and resources to make its site top-notch in terms of the loading speed. The "framed" page of yours, on the other hand, can take its sweet time to load after the Amazon page has completed loading. This could leave an impression that your book description field is completely empty and disappoints impatient visitors who don't wait around.

c) SSL concern. Many of the Amazon family sites, amazon.co.uk and amazon.de etc, tend to serve off SSL secure layer (following the https: protocol instead of the http: protocol. If your external page cannot be accessed via https – many small Web sites do not bother acquiring an SSL certificate and therefore cannot be served off SSL layer – the iframe on your book page can look like the following screenshot when the Amazon host page is served off SSL:

This Connection is Untrusted

You have asked Firefox to connect securely to **everydayfiction.com**, but we can't confirm that your connection is secure.

Normally, when you try to connect securely, sites will present trusted identification to prove that you are going to the right place. However, this site's identity can't be verified.

What Should I Do?

If you usually connect to this site without problems, this error could mean that someone is trying to impersonate the site, and you shouldn't continue.

Get me out of here!

Technical Details

Psychologically, this could easily lessen a prospective buyer's interest toward your book.

My recommendation is to keep iFrames to the bare minimum. Use one when you really have a compelling reason, not just for the sake of ease and the freedom it affords you.

Where to place JavaScript code blocks

Now that you have an exciting and beautiful book description on your book page, you may have forgotten how the same HTML description block looks inside your Amazon AuthorCentral Book List. Using the same example as used in Chapter Five, we can refresh our memory of how the raw HTML description block looks inside AuthorCentral:

Product Description   Edit

About the author: M. Eigh is just another harmless Asian dude who makes a quiet livir beautiful wife, two daughters and two cats in a charming old house, which came with mortgage. He dreams of murdering that landlord with a bestseller someday, preferably colleges. His hermit kingdom is at <a href="//m.eigh.com">m.eigh.com</a>. <br clear= /wp-content/Mrk_by_Shiloh_Penfield.jpg" border="0" align="left" />
A picture is \ Sullivan, one of the main victims of Troma in <i>The Cicada Survival Guide</i>, by Sh it take to bring down an elevator in an apartment building? Can a deadly cicada turn huge swarm of Brood II cicadas attack a CIA Deputy Director on the steps of the Cap they carriers of something lethal?
Do you want to know why the government ha attipt to wipe the cicadas out? Do you even know how to defend yourself with Taser <i>The Cicada Survival Guide</i> today.

For those brave enough, a victor Delicious and battle-tested cicada recipes included!

Lori Milani, a.k.a. "Cic WashingtonPost special on Cicada on May 18. {<a href="//bit.ly/109Q621" target="_b CicadaPhobia</a>} Lori did an extensiveinterview with the author on May 30. For tho: conceived, please hop over CicadaPhobia's site and readthe interview. { <a href="//bi Interviews M. Eigh</a>)<br clear="all"/><h2>Do you say si-KAY-da? Or si-KAH-da? W </h2><div align="center"><iframe width="640" height="360" src="//youtube.com/emb frameborder="0" allowfullscreen></iframe></div><script type="text/javascript" src="// type="text/javascript">${document).ready(function(){amz_expandPostBodyDescriptio </script><br clear="all"/><br clear="all"/><h2>Read a recently published short fiction align="center"><dframe src="//everydayfiction.com/oscars-ten-commandments-by-m- </div><br clear="all"/><br clear="all"/><div align="center"><h2>Other titles by M. Eigh type="text/javascript" src="//ws-na.amazon-adsystem.com/widgets/q?rt=tf_ssw&Ser ID=V20070822%2FUS%2Fmei0cc-20%2f8003%2Fc334e494-c210-453c-a426-74153e </SCRIPT> <NOSCRIPT><A HREF="//ws-na.amazon-adsystem.com/widgets/q?rt=tf_s/

Well, definitely not pretty. But we don't care, since we think the only place this block is going to be seen is in the Amazon book page, where it will be rendered beautifully. But are we sure?

It turns out that the same "raw" view is displayed on Facebook when you share your book's link. Somehow Facebook follows Amazon's API and fetches a book's description from the same source as Amazon's Web servers, except it renders the snippet verbatim, without interpreting them into HTML tags.

The above example will look like this on a typical wall post:

Whew! Thank the gods that my code gibberish is pretty low down the line; otherwise they would be there verbatim and looking like a careless error.

The moral of the lesson, of course, is to keep the pure function-centric JavaScript code as close to the HTML description block as possible.

Lex parsimoniae and white spaces in the HTML description

When you are enhancing your book description with widgets and videos, the functional JavaScript code snippets themselves consume a big chunk of the 4000-character quota. Often, it is likely that you find it impossible to squeeze into the description field all that you want to say about your book, because the fancy JavaScript snippets have taken up a lot of characters.

Those are the moments you need to exercise *lex parsimoniae* and get rid of all unnecessary white spaces in your HTML block. White spaces can be double encoded as " " as a result, a single white space can become a whopping six-character string. For example, both of the following two HTML snippets are valid:

Version A:

```
<p>I am a book.</p>
<p>I have a beautiful cover.</p>
```

Version B:

```
<p>I am a book.</p><p>I have a
beautiful cover.</p>
```

Except Version A may cost you many character allowances. Remember, you are dealing with a code block and Version A and Version B do not result in any different rendering, so why not just go with Version B so that no character allowances are wasted?

Getting rid of unnecessary white spaces also helps prevent accidental line breaks. In principle, your entire HTML description block should be in *one* single line. This keeps thing tidy and when you get the block HTML encoded (double encoded,) line breaks are often the culprits that breaks your code.

So remember, no line breaks, no unnecessary white spaces.

How fancy can you get with JavaScript in your book description?

The answer is simple: Sky's the limit. If a widget can fly on a Web page, it can be added to your book description page.

In some of my books, I've embedded a JavaScript-generated slideshow. You can find an example of my slideshow under the Description of my illustration book *My Life as a Cicada* (http://amzn.to/15ZnnLZ.) The same slideshow is also used to demonstrate the power of JavaScript in full HTML book description this book's description field.

Now, I will give you a quick walk through on this slideshow. You are welcome to use the exact code for a slideshow of yours. But I would prefer that you reference this as an example.

a)   First off, any JavaScript widgets, or jQuery widgets as jQuery has become synonymous to JavaScript these days, rely on CSS and JavaScript definitions to render an HTML block. These definitions could be quite sizable and in no ways can they ever fit into a book description field that only allows 4,000 characters. So in my case, I have consolidated all CSS definition related to the slideshow into one single file c.sss. I've also aggregated all the JavaScript functional code into one single file e.js and its dependent jQuery definition as j.js. I use as short a name to reference an external file because the length of its name counts against my 4,000 character limit. I reference these three files as follows:

```
<link type="text/css"
rel="stylesheet" media="all"
href="//googledrive.com/host/0B6N
osDCPlbuIZzN4MS1hU2hHZjQ/c.css"
/><script type="text/JavaScript"
src="//googledrive.com/host/0B6No
sDCPlbuIZzN4MS1hU2hHZjQ/j.js"></s
cript><script
type="text/JavaScript"
src="//googledrive.com/host/0B6No
sDCPlbuIZzN4MS1hU2hHZjQ/e.js">
```

b) After that, I put all my image references inside a Div bearing theID of myGallery so that my JavaScript and CSS know which element in my book description HTML block they should work on, as follows:

```
<div id="myGallery"
class="spacegallery"><img
src="//pbs.twimg.com/media/BTzkMZ
-CcAE_27B.jpg" alt="" /><img
src="//pbs.twimg.com/media/BTzkk0
-CEAAc4tC.jpg" alt="" /><img
src="//pbs.twimg.com/media/BTzk8t
xCIAAlK92.jpg" alt="" /><img
src="//pbs.twimg.com/media/BTzpB2
jCcAAmdkz.jpg" alt="" /><img
src="//pbs.twimg.com/media/BTzpaS
ZCYAIy2l3.jpg" alt="" /><img
src="//pbs.twimg.com/media/BTzp0h
GCEAEFVJ7.jpg" alt="" /></div>
```

If you are very perceptive and careful, you would probably have noticed that my CSS, JavaScript or image files are either placed on the servers of Google or Twitter. The rationale behind it is explained in Chapter Eleven. For now, just take my word for it: It is much better to leverage these big guys' charity than hosting these files on your own servers.

c) Finally, I need to tell my referenced JavaScript file e.js when exactly to fire up all the functions defined in it. Execution cannot be too early as JavaScript basically manipulates HTML elements. It cannot do so before the elements have been loaded by a browser. By the same token, it cannot be too late. If the slideshow functional JavaScript executes too late, the users will see the slideshow but find it unanimated and unclickable. The perfect moment to fire up the slideshow related JavaScript is when all the elements fully load on the page. This is when we find jQuery handy. With jQuery's $(document).ready(); call, we can time everything to execute at that right moment:

```
<script
type="text/JavaScript">$(document
).ready(function(){$('#myGallery'
).spacegallery({loadingClass:
'loading'});});</script>
```

The result is what you see on this book's description page.

In a nutshell, the steps we have taken to get the slideshow working in my book description is generally applicable when you put a JavaScript (or jQuery) widget in your book description.

And as a rule of thumb, if you can make a JavaScript widget work in an HTML page, it will work in an Amazon book description field. The only difference is when you have it working in an HTML page, the code you put in is as-is. But with an Amazon book description field, the same block of code used in that HTML page must be double-encoded or HTML encoded, as explained in details in Chapter Five.

I am sure that if you wrap your mind around it and apply the principle and guideline I have described above, you will come up with more innovative and inspiring ways to construct your own book description, by way of HTML and JavaScript.

And if you have an JavaScript widget that is already working in an HTML page but you cannot get it to work in your Amazon book description field, check to make sure you have followed the steps outlined in Chapter Five.

If you believe that you have followed the instructions outlined in Chapter Five but still could not get it to work, please shoot me an email. If you do not have my email already, please use the Question on "KDP's Best-Kept Secret Revealed" form in this book's description to contact me.

Good luck!

Chapter Eleven: How to Leverage CDN in Your Book Description

For those who do not know, CDN stands for Content Delivery Network. It is exclusively a Big Boys' Game. The Web servers of internet giants such as Google, Facebook and Twitter as well as Amazon all have great performance, backed by their CDN-optimized hardware and bandwidth. There is just no chance that your own Website host's servers can outperform them. They are also much more reliable than your own Website host. And if that does not convince you yet, think about geo-optimized server performance a CDN can provide, as opposed to your own Website host that is only optimized for your home base, be it North American, Europe or Asia.

So, if you are with me on that, you would choose to put your book trailers on YouTube, your pictures on Google Drive or Twitter. I do not recommend Flickr or any other Yahoo family services, simply because they tend to change terms of service a lot. If your book description is tied to images used in your free Flickr account and Yahoo all of a sudden changes the quota allowance for free account, your intended pictures may show up blank on your book page.

Another compelling reason to use CDN for your files has to do with the SSL concern we talked about in Chapter Ten, on the subject of iFrames. If your files are stored on a server that does not have a SSL certificate, the images, CSS and JavaScript cannot be delivered to the visitors' browsers if they are visiting an Amazon site under the https: protocol, as they often do for sites like Amazon.de and Amazon.co.uk. When that happens, your book page breaks and your hard work of putting together a fancy description backfires. CDN such as Google Drive and Twitter, on the other hand, serve their content via the normal http and the secure https protocol with the same robust performance. Plus it doesn't cost you anything as an SSL certificate will.

Let's walk through two examples of getting your pictures hosted on Twitter and Google Drive.

1) How to get your picture hosted by Twitter:

    a) First, include a picture in your Tweet:

    b) Right-click on the picture you've just Tweeted and choose "Copy Image Location" from the context menu:

c)   Paste the location into a text editor:

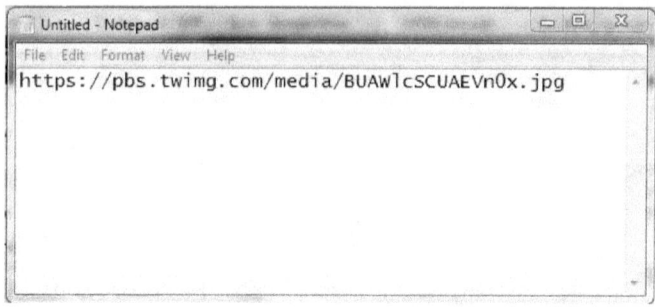

In my case I've got the following URL for the image:

```
https://pbs.twimg.com/media/BUAWlcSCUAE
VnOx.jpg
```

Which is all and well. However, if I need to use it in an HTML img tag and include in my book description, I have to remember, once again, to chop off the "http:" part of the url string:

```
//pbs.twimg.com/media/BUAWlcSCUAEVnOx.j
pg
```

2)   How to get your picture hosted by Google Drive

Most people know how to use Google Drive as an equivalent of local file folder on your computer, but few people know that Google Drive can serve as a Web server and deliver your files online. This is very handy for images, CSS, JavaScript and other file types you need to deliver online with reliable performance and no cost to you. While Twitter is equally as good, it cannot hold your CSS, JavaScript or PDF's. This basically answers the question some of you may have had when reading Chapter Ten and wondering why my CSS and JavaScript files are all stored on Google Drive.

Without further ado, let's get the same picture used in the Twitter hosting example into Google Drive.

 a) Log into your Google Drive account. If you have never used it before, create a Gmail account for yourself and log in and click on "Drive" from the top navigation bar. Once you log in, create a new folder under "My Drive:"

 b) Give it a name that reminds of its purpose:

c) In your Drive view, check the box next to the folder you have just created and click on the More button and choose to share:

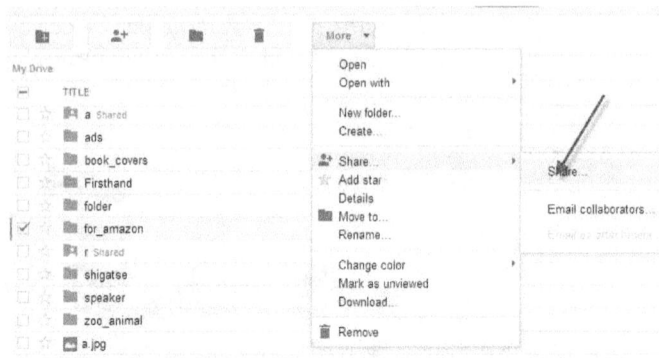

d) Google Drive will now prompt you to change the folder's share permission:

e) Click on "Change" and select "Public on the Web" and click on "Save:"

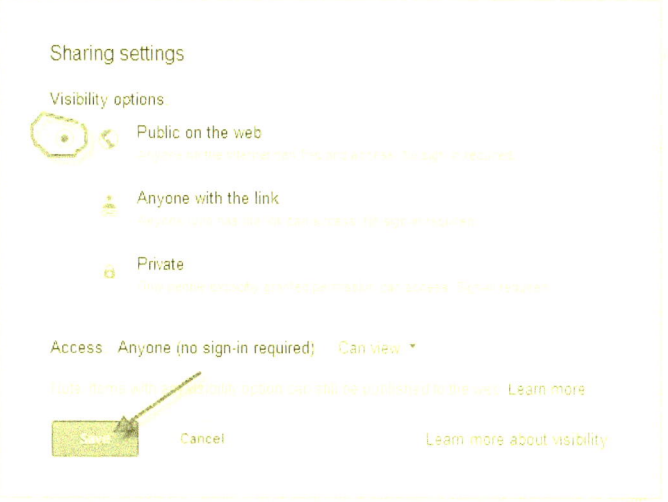

f) You have now effectively turned your Drive folder as a Web server folder and given the world read access. Copy the "Link to share" somewhere safe and easily retrievable:

g) Of the "Link to share" URL, we are "id" string:

https://drive.google.com/folderview?id=0B6NosDCP
1buIT0tubFN3QkV3ZXc&usp=sharing

h) Now click this folder to expand it and upload the picture in question into this folder, confirming "Upload and share" to Google Drive:

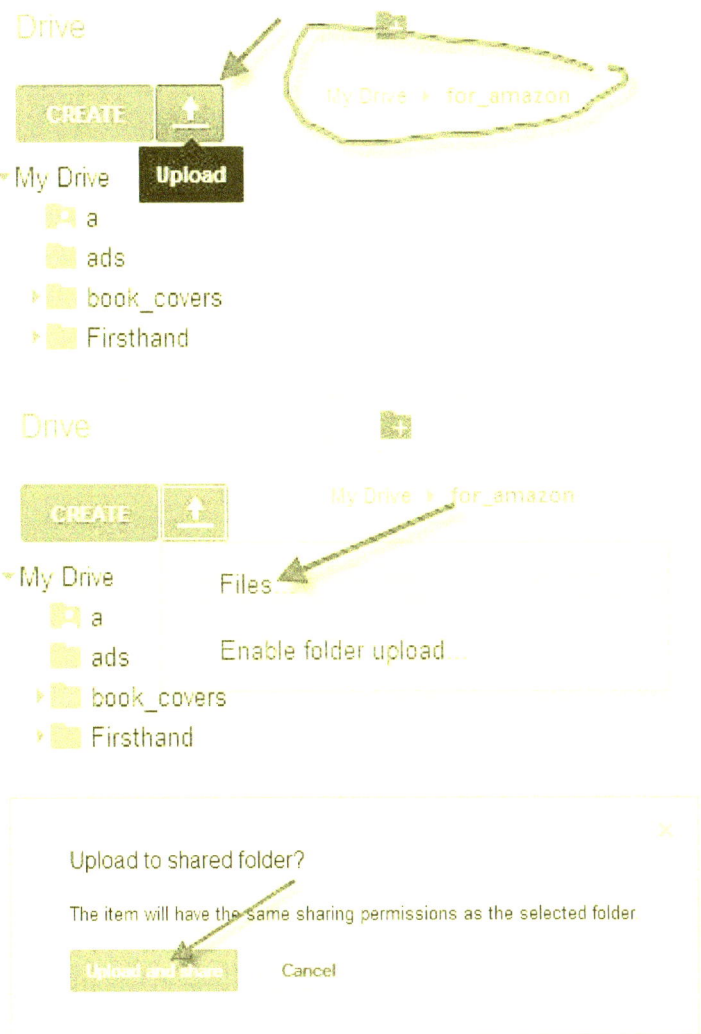

i) Now the file appears in my folder and is clearly marked as "Shared." The only way the general

public can view a picture in your book
description that is hosted in Google Drive is if
it is shared. Now we notice that I have given
the file a ridiculously long name, which does
not play well with Amazon's book description
field. This filename wastes too many of my
character quota, so I select it and proceed to
rename it:

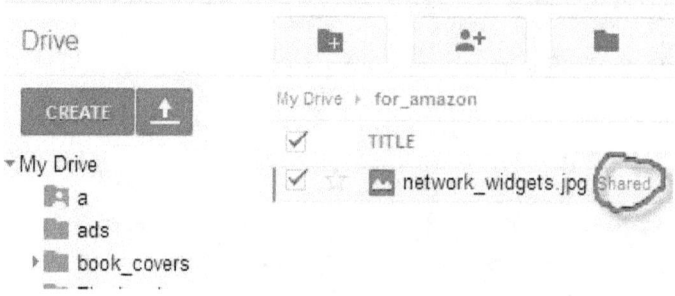

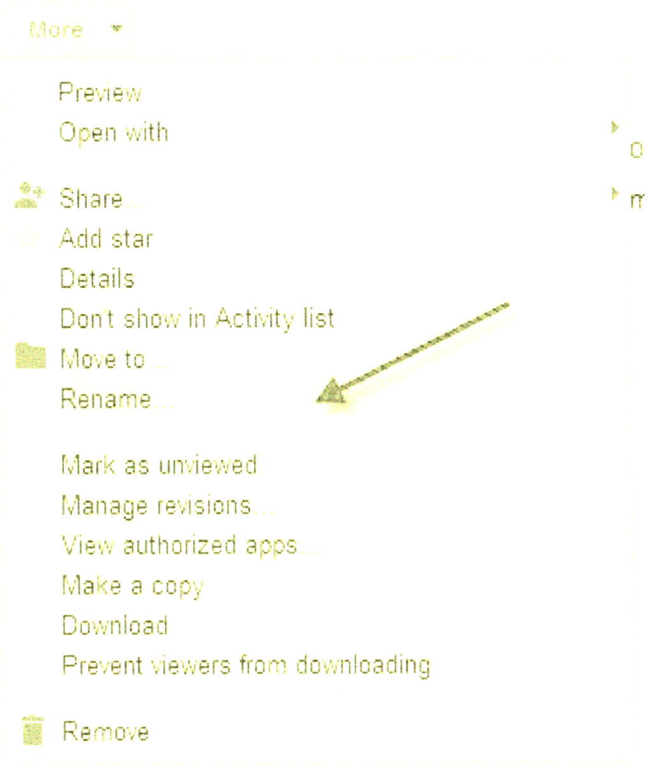

More ▾

Preview
Open with   ▸ o

Share   ▸ m
Add star
Details
Don t show in Activity list
Move to
Rename

Mark as unviewed
Manage revisions
View authorized apps
Make a copy
Download
Prevent viewers from downloading

Remove

Rename

Please enter a new name for the item

n.jpg

OK   Cancel

j) Now we will test viewing the file from the Web, to make sure that it is accessible by the general public. This is the moment we need to use the folder id we saved earlier. All files in that folder will bear a URL pattern as follows:

https://googledrive.com/host/id/filename

So the picture's URL will be as follows:

```
https://googledrive.com/host/0B6N
osDCPlbuIT0tubFN3QkV3ZXc/n.jpg
```

(Caution: the public facing Google Drive servers use a different domain. It is googledrive.com, not drive.google.com or docs.google.com.)

In order to truly test the file's accessibility, you either need to log out of your Drive account or use a different browser.

3) Google Drive vs. Twitter

As I mentioned earlier, Google Drive and Twitter are equally good free service for you to deliver your files to your book description.

When the file types are PDF, zip, CSS and JavaScript, the natural choice is Google Drive and there is no question about it. But when it comes to images, you do have the choice.

Other than personal preference, here are the pros and cons concerning Google Drive and Twitter:

a) Google Drive's file URLs are longer than that of Twitters, due largely to the length of the folder id (32 characters.) When you are pressed for space in your book description, you would naturally choose Twitter for your pictures as their URLs are going to be shorter and take up fewer character allowances.

b) Twitter randomizes your pictures filename and the URLs, compared to that of Google Drive's, are unpredictable. If you have many image assets used in your book description and you have a specific nomenclature to govern the collection, Google Drive can maintain the fidelity of your filenames while Twitter cannot. So when you are not pressed for space in your description field, Google Drive appears to be the clear choice.

Chapter Twelve: How to Leverage Social Media in Your Book Description

Amazon is very draconian in segregating the buyers from the sellers. Other than the reviews a few of your buyers post on your books, you as authors do not really have any effective means to interact with your readers. Many KDP authors and self publishers struggle with this aspect of Amazon and get frustrated.

As a result, you see many authors attempt to leave their emails, Twitter handles or Facebook urls in the book description or About the Author fields, in plain text format. That is the best they can do.

But people are lazy by nature, if they have to select a block of text and copy into their browsers' address in order to view your Twitter or Facebook page, they never bother. If they have to copy your email address and turn the disguise of [at] into an @ sign and a [dot] into a dot, they simply lose interest. But they will click on something if it is right there. That's why I embed my Tweet box and a Facebook Post box in my About the Author field. (You can do it in the Description field if you so choose, or the Editorial Review field. It's a matter of marketing strategy and maximizing the use of character allowances.)

1) Embedding a Tweet box in a book field.
    a) The first step is to obtain the block of HTML and JavaScript code that comes from your Twitter account. After you log into your Twitter account, browse to https://twitter.com/settings/widgets and you will get to option to create your own widget:

b) You will have choices to create different kinds of widgets but that is completely out of scope with this book. For demonstration purposes, I will use the "Tweets by M. Eigh (@m_eigh)" widget I have already created for myself. Once you click on "Edit," you will be able to see how the widget looks and copy its code:

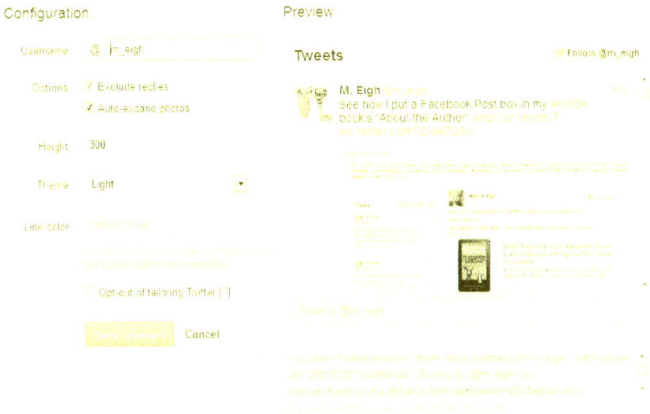

c) For my Tweet box I get the following code:

```
<a class="twitter-timeline"
href="https://twitter.com/m_eigh"
data-widget-
id="289132321204998144">Tweets by
@m_eigh</a>
```

```
<script>!function(d,s,id){var
js,fjs=d.getElementsByTagName(s)[
0],p=/^http:/.test(d.location)?'h
ttp':'https';if(!d.getElementById
(id)){js=d.createElement(s);js.id
=id;js.src=p+"://platform.twitter
.com/widgets.js";fjs.parentNode.i
nsertBefore(js,fjs);}}(document,"
script","twitter-wjs");</script>
```

This is when things get tricky. In general, all HTML block of any social media widget must be treated verbatim when you input them into KDP book field. On the contrary, all JavaScript block cannot be treated verbatim. In fact, almost all of them must be rewritten. It is an interpretative re-write in principle. And there is no cheat sheet or formula to follow. You either know how to read JavaScript and replace the highlighted block with a more straightforward, Amazon book field friendly JavaScript equivalent, or you just have to work with someone who knows JavaScript well enough to get it done.

Although there may be exception, I can say most of Twitter widget's JavaScript block can be simply substituted with the following simple reference:

```
<script
src="//platform.twitter.com/widge
ts.js"></script>
```

And you can't get simpler than that. So my Tweet box widget code, HTML plus JavaScript, becomes as follows:

```
<a class="twitter-timeline"
href="https://twitter.com/m_eigh"
data-widget-
id="289132321204998144">Tweets by
@m_eigh</a><script
src="//platform.twitter.com/widge
ts.js"></script>
```

After this all I need to do is follow the steps outlined in Chapter Five to input the following block into a book field.

For review purposes, let's do a quick walk through to remind ourselves of the steps:

(1) Log into AuthorCentral, locate the book from your Book List, select the Kindle format and click on Edit on the field you wish to operate.

(2) Make sure you are working with the Compose tab of the text Editor.

(3) Double encode or HTML-encode the above Twitter widget code before you paste it into the Editor.

(4) Click on "Preview" to watch it get decoded into the original HTML and JavaScript.

(5) Click on Save and wait for about 30 minutes.

Voila, there I have my Tweet box live on Amazon:

About the Author

M. Eigh is just another Asian dude who
morbidly obese landlord, also known as th
kingdom is at m.eigh.com

2) Embedding a Facebook box in a book field.

Like Twitter, Facebook offers many widgets. The
creation of those widget falls outside the scope of this
book. For demonstration purposes, I am using a
Facebook Post box widget which ties specifically with
one of my post.

a) Visit Facebook's social plugin page at https://developers.facebook.com/docs/plugins/. From the left nave choose "Embedded posts."

facebook developers

Social Plugins

Like Button

Send Button

Embedded Posts

Follow Button

Comments

Share Dialog

Activity Feed

Recommendations Box

Recommendations Bar

Like Box

Login Button

Registration

Facepile

b) Once I supply my Facebook post's URL, the widget becomes live:

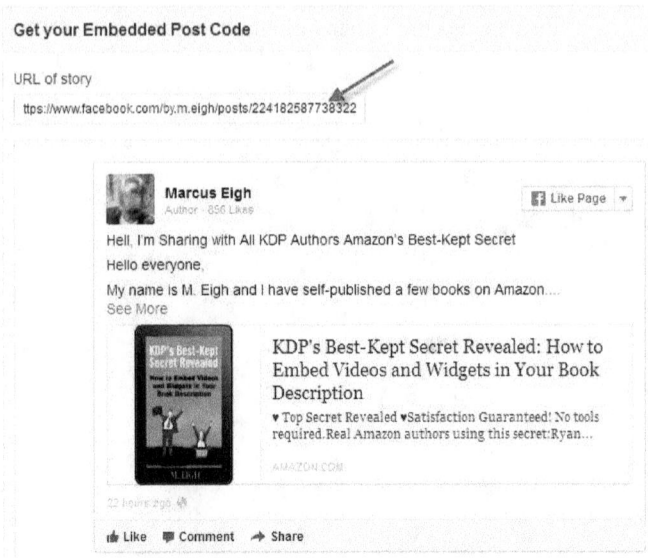

c) Click on the "Get Code" and you will be presented with the code block. Make sure that the HTML5 tab is active. Other formats work as well but for the purpose of embedding the widget into Amazon's book field, HTML5 is the most suitable:

```
Your Plugin Code

  HTML5   XFBML   IFRAME   URL

Include the JavaScript SDK on your page once ideally right after the opening <body> tag

  <div id="fb-root"></div>
  <script> function d, s, id) {
    var js, fjs = d.getElementsByTagName(s)[0];
    if (d.getElementById(id)) return;
    js = d.createElement(s); js.id = id;
    js.src = "//connect.facebook.net/en_US/all.js#xfbml=1";
    fjs.parentNode.insertBefore(js, fjs);
  } document, 'script', 'facebook-jssdk'));</script>

Place the code for your plugin wherever you want the plugin to appear on your page

  <div class="fb-post" data-href="https://www.facebook.com/by.m.eigh/posts/224182587738322">
  </div>
```

You have probably noticed that Facebook's widget code, just like that of Twitter, features simple HTML but fairly convoluted JavaScript:

```
<div class="fb-post" data-href="
//www.facebook.com/by.m.eigh/posts/2241
82587738322"></div>
<div id="fb-root"></div>
<script>(function(d, s, id) {
   var js, fjs =
d.getElementsByTagName(s)[0];
   if (d.getElementById(id)) return;
   js = d.createElement(s); js.id = id;
   js.src =
"//connect.facebook.net/en_US/all.js#xfbml
=1";
   fjs.parentNode.insertBefore(js, fjs);
  }(document, 'script', 'facebook-
jssdk'));</script>
```

Once again, we are forced to interpret and re-write the code. Just like in the case of Twitter, for most of Facebook's widgets, their JavaScript block can be simply replaced with the following one:

```
<script
src"//connect.facebook.net/en_US/all.js#xf
bml=1"></script>
```

So treating the HTML portion of the code verbatim and incorporating our own re-written JavaScript, we have our Facebook Post Box code put together as follows:

```
<div class="fb-post" data-href="
//www.facebook.com/by.m.eigh/posts/2241
82587738322"></div>
<div id="fb-root"></div>
<script
src="//connect.facebook.net/en_US/all.js#x
fbml=1"></script>
```

From here on we just need to follow the same procedure as we did for the Twitter widget (which is also detailed in Chapter Five.) And voila, we have the Facebook Post Box in a book field:

About the Author

M. Eigh is just another Asian dude who makes a quiet living in IT. He lives in Northern Virginia with his beautiful wife, two daughters morbidly obese landlord, also known as the mortgage. He dreams of murdering that landlord with a bestseller someday, preferably befo kingdom is at m.eigh.com

Caution: If you have not noticed, let me point it out to you: Every step of the way throughout the above process, I have vigilantly stripped off the "http:" or "https:" part of a URL. By default, all the URLs in the code block you obtain from Twitter or Facebook contains such strings. Do not forget to strip them off, or else your widget cannot be rendered in your book page.

3)   Embedding social share buttons in a book field.

For demonstration purposes, I am using AddThis as my social share buttons provider. They have been around for a long time and their code seems to have worked out all the kinks and their servers' performance seems to be quite good. But there are many different varieties and flavors of social share buttons and you can pick whatever kind that tickles your fancy to implement. They pretty much work in the same fashion, so the following steps taken to get AddThis buttons into my book description field can be followed in the same way.

The only litmus test you have to conduct, is to test a button provider's ability to service the buttons over SSL (when the browsers use https: instead of plain http: to access Amazon's sites, as often happens with Amazon's sites outside North America.)

For example, ShareThis®, offers free share buttons at http://www.sharethis.com/get-sharing-tools/#sthash.JToaWJ7m.dpbs. When I choose "Websites," I get a block of code representing a beautiful slab of buttons as shown below:

Preview

HTML:

```
<span class='st_sharethis_large'
displayText='ShareThis'></span>
<span class='st_facebook_large'
displayText='Facebook'></span>
<span class='st_twitter_large'
displayText='Tweet'></span>
<span class='st_linkedin_large'
displayText='LinkedIn'></span>
<span class='st_pinterest_large'
displayText='Pinterest'></span>
<span class='st_email_large'
displayText='Email'></span>
```

Javascript:

```
<script type="text/javascript">var
switchTo5x=true;</script>
<script type="text/javascript"
src="http://w.sharethis.com/button/butt
ons.js"></script>
<script
type="text/javascript">stLight.options(
{publisher: "398c8327-9f37-4c1e-bfc3-
a934d76846bd", doNotHash: false,
doNotCopy: false, hashAddressBar:
false});</script>
```

The key element, the SDK Javascript file, is located at http://w.sharethis.com/button/buttons.js.

Now let's conduct a routine litmus test by accessing the SDK file via SSL. To do that, we try to load https://w.sharethis.com/button/buttons.js in a browser. Immediately, we get SSL warning. In Firefox, the warning looks like this:

This Connection is Untrusted

You have asked Firefox to connect securely to **w.sharethis.com**, but we can't confirm that your connection is secure.

Normally, when you try to connect securely, sites will present trusted identification to prove that you are going to the right place. However, this site's identity can't be verified.

What Should I Do?

If you usually connect to this site without problems, this error could mean that someone is trying to impersonate the site, and you shouldn't continue.

Get me out of here!

Technical Details

I Understand the Risks

While ShareThis buttons maybe perfectly good enough for your WordPress blog which does not have any eCommerce capability and you never have to use SSL, you must remember that you are now trying to put these buttons into your Kindle book page, which is served off Amazon's website, a primary eCommerce market place, where browsers are frequently forced to exchange data with Amazon's servers through SSL.

So ShareThis and its ilk who cannot deliver their SDK over SSL and therefore cannot be accommodated in your Kindle book page.

Now let's try AddThis. We now proceed to AddThis and click on "Get Code" and we are presented with a configuration page at
`https://www.addthis.com/get/smart-layers#.UjU0NT_9UY0`:

Get the Code

▸ Follow   OFF

▸ Share   ON

▸ What's Next   OFF

▸ Recommended Content   OFF

▾ More Options

We will turn everything off except "Share." Remember, these buttons will live on Amazon's page, not your own blog and you do not have any of your personal profile plugged in that page. All you will ever care is for the visitors to share the page's URL with their friends and family.

With that in mind, we click on the "Generate Code" button and grab the code:

We then pick out AddThis's SDK file at
http://s7.addthis.com/js/300/addthis_widge
t.js and test it over SSL by accessing
https://s7.addthis.com/js/300/addthis_widg
et.js in a browser. No problem. So AddThis passes the
litmus test.

Next comes the tricky task of entering the above code
snippet into your Kindle book description. This is not an
intuitive process, and you must follow the steps outlined as
follows to get the entry done. Any deviation, intentional or
accidental, may result in the social share buttons' failure to
render and leaving unreadable gibberish in your book
description.

After stripping off all the unnecessary comments and
linebreaks, I get the code for AddThis social share buttons:

```
<script
src="//s7.addthis.com/js/300/addthis_widge
t.js#pubid=ra-
5234a9952b2c4543"></script><script
type="text/javascript">addthis.layers({'th
eme' : 'transparent','share' :
{'position' :
'right','numPreferredServices' :
5} });</script>
```

From here on the steps are:

(1) Log into AuthorCentral, locate the book from your Book List, select the Kindle format and click on Edit on the Product Description field you wish to operate. It is very important to understand that social share buttons can *only* be embedded in the Kindle format version of your book. It does not work inside the book description of your paperback or other format versions.

Books › My Mother's Shadow ⌄

My Mother's Shadow
Kindle Edition

ASIN: B00ERCS7ZM
Average Review: ☆☆☆☆☆ (2 reviews)
Current Sales Rank: #241,792 in Kindle Store
View on Amazon.com ⌁

| Editorial Reviews | Book Details | Book Extras |

Review   [Edit]

<h2>Praises</h2>"(<i>My Mother's Shadow</i> is) a truly beautiful piece of story, each interesting enough to mull over for some time.

I was contain no blatant description you understand the conflict and empathize wit other literary references.<h2>★★★★ --Alain Gomez, <i>Book Brouhaha</i></ discovers that this is a curse from God ...<h2>★★★★★ -- Grady Harp, HALL the consequences of being born without a shadow. It was eerily reminiscent REVIEWER</h2>One of the the most interesting stories that took place in the have always admired those that can contain their creativity within the limite the short form.<h2>★★★★★ -- Ghauger</h2>

Product Description   [Edit]

<table border="0" cellspacing="0" cellpadding="10"><tbody><tr><td colspan= most recent book, <a href="/dp/B00F23Q9CI"><i>KDP's Best-Kept Secret Rev of the Town among Indie writers and self-publishers. If you are publishing or out</a>. His hermit kingdom is at <a href="//m.eigh.com">m.eigh.com</a></ id="289132321204998144">Tweets by @m_eigh</a><script src="//platform.t /by.m.eigh/posts/224182587738322"></div><div id="fb-root"></div><script s child is born shadowless into a world ruled by those with shadow. She's grow

   (2) Make sure you are working with the Compose tab of the text Editor. *Do not* use the HTML tab.

What "Product Description" should not include:

- Spoilers! please don't reveal crucial plot elements.
- Phone numbers, mail addresses, URLs.

Important: Once you make a change to a section here, your publisher will not be able to make any further changes to the same section. If you are a Kindle Direct Publishing author, and you make changes to your Product Description here, you will no longer be able to make edits via KDP.

More details on "Product Description" guidelines here .

Format: **B** *I* ≟≡ ☷

```
<table border="0" cellspacing="0" cellpadding="10"><tbody><tr><td colspan="2"><h2
style="display:inline">M. Eigh</h2> is just another Asian dude who makes a quiet living in IT. His
most recent book, <a href=" dp B00F23Q9C1"><i>KDP's Best-Kept Secret Revealed: How to
Embed Videos and Widgets in Your Book Description</i></a> is a bestseller and the Talk of the
Town among Indie writers and self-publishers. If you are publishing or ever want to publish Kindle
books, you owe it to yourself to <a href=" dp B00F23Q9C1">check it out</a>. His hermit kingdom
is at <a href=" m eigh com">m eigh com</a></td></tr><tr><td width="20%"><a class="twitter-
timeline" href="twitter.com m_eigh" data-widget-id="289132321204998144">Tweets by
@m_eigh</a><script src=" platform.twitter.com widgets js"></script></td><td width="80%"><div
class="fb-post" data-href=" facebook.com by m eigh posts 224182587738322"></div><div
id="fb-root"></div><script src=" connect facebook net en US all js#xfbml=1"></script>
```

are tons of free HTML encoders available online for you to download and install on your computer or device. As a matter of fact, since the HTML code block you are using for Book Description is guaranteed to be small (Amazon imposes a 4000 character limit on the Description field,) the easiest way to get the HTML encoding process done is to find a online HTML encoder and do it through a Web form. If you just Google "online HTML encoder," you should be able to find many choices. But my favorite is located at http://www.opinionatedgeek.com/DotNet/Tools/HTMLEncode/Encode.aspx. The following screenshot shows you how an entire book description HTML block gets double encoded with this online encoder:

Type or paste in the text you want to HTML encode, then press the 'Encode' button, or read a brief explanation of the process of HTML encoding.

Encode input text:

```
<script
src="//s7.addthis.com/js/300/addthis_widget.js#
pubid=ra-5234a9952b2c4543"></script><script
type="text/javascript">addthis.layers
({'theme' : 'transparent','share' :
{'position' : 'right','numPreferredServices' :
5} });</script>
```

Don't forget to check out out online HTML Decoder.

Encode

Encoded Output

Here is the HTML-encoded output:

```
&lt;script
src=&quot;//s7.addthis.com/js/300/addthis_widge
t.js#pubid=ra-
5234a9952b2c4543&quot;&gt;&lt;/script&gt;&lt;sc
ript
type=&quot;text/javascript&quot;&gt;addthis.lay
ers({&#39;theme&#39; :
&#39;transparent&#39;,&#39;share&#39; :
{&#39;position&#39; :
&#39;right&#39;,&#39;numPreferredServices&#39;
: 5} });&lt;/script&gt;
```

After the aforementioned double encoding process, I get a block of completely unreadable character soup as shown below. Do not be concerned. The share buttons has just got a Amazon-friendly make-over.

```
&lt;script
src=&quot;//s7.addthis.com/js/
300/addthis_widget.js#pubid=ra
-
5234a9952b2c4543&quot;&gt;&lt;
/script&gt;&lt;script
type=&quot;text/javascript&quo
t;&gt;addthis.layers({&#39;the
me&#39; :
&#39;transparent&#39;,&#39;sha
re&#39; : {&#39;position&#39; :
&#39;right&#39;,&#39;numPrefer
redServices&#39; :
5} });&lt;/script&gt;
```

Paste the above gibberish block into the compose window. Try your best to not introduce any white space or linebreaks, both of which can damage the integrity of the code snippet and render it completely useless. The snippet will look insane. But that is the way it should look at this stage:

Important: Once you make a change to a section here, your publisher will not be able to make any further changes to the same section. If you are a Kindle Direct Publishing author, and you make changes to your Product Description here, you will no longer be able to make edits via KDP.

More details on "Product Description" guidelines here .

Format: **B** *I* ≣ ≣

<script src=" s".addthis.com js 300 addthis_widget.js=pubid=ra-5234a9952b2c4543&
quot;>< script><script type="text javascript">addthis.layers({&=39;
theme&=39; :&=39;transparent&=39,,&=39;share&=39; : {&=39;position&=39; :
&=39;right&=39;,&=39;numPreferredServices&=39; : 5} }),< script>

Preview

(4) Click on "Preview" to watch it get decoded into the original HTML and JavaScript.

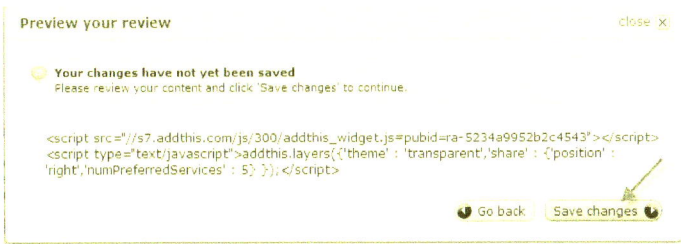

Preview your review   close ×

Your changes have not yet been saved
Please review your content and click 'Save changes' to continue.

```
<script src="//s7.addthis.com/js/300/addthis_widget.js=pubid=ra-5234a9952b2c4543"></script>
<script type="text/javascript">addthis.layers({'theme' : 'transparent','share' : {'position' :
'right','numPreferredServices' : 5} });</script>
```

Go back   Save changes

(5) Click on Save and wait for about 30 minutes.

And voila, we have the Social Share Buttons floating on the right edge of the book page:

Afterthoughts

If you have read this book, chances are that you yourself are a KDP author or publisher, and that you are familiar with that dreadful silence when someone reads your book but does not say a thing afterwards.

I am eager to hear from you. Good or bad, please give me your honest critique. And share your story with other readers. If this book has helped you in any humble manner, please mention it. Your satisfaction is my gratification.

By the same token, if you have a complaint or find inadequacy in this book, drop me a line or even complain in a book review you post. I will push out a revision of expansion to address the issue. I would like you to benefit from this book to the very maximum. But I cannot achieve that without your help.

So help me by posting an honest review. Or if you rather stay out of the public light, drop me a note at eigh.com@gmail.com, I will more than happy to correspond with you.

To post a review, please go to http://amzn.to/1evdevT.

Thank you again for purchasing and reading this book. It means a ton to me.

www.ingramcontent.com/pod-product-compliance
Lightning Source LLC
Chambersburg PA
CBHW051337170526
45166CB00002B/856